D0930950

The Kentucky Bicentennial Bookshelf
Sponsored by

KENTUCKY HISTORICAL EVENTS CELEBRATION COMMISSION
KENTUCKY FEDERATION OF WOMEN'S CLUBS

and Contributing Sponsors

AMERICAN FEDERAL SAVINGS & LOAN ASSOCIATION
ARMCO STEEL CORPORATION, ASHLAND WORKS
A. ARNOLD & SON TRANSFER & STORAGE CO., INC. / ASHLAND OIL, INC.
BAILEY MINING COMPANY, BYPRO, KENTUCKY / BEGLEY DRUG COMPANY
J. WINSTON COLEMAN, JR. / CONVENIENT INDUSTRIES OF AMERICA, INC.
IN MEMORY OF MR. AND MRS. J. SHERMAN COOPER BY THEIR CHILDREN
CORNING GLASS WORKS FOUNDATION / MRS. CLORA CORRELL
THE COURIER-JOURNAL AND THE LOUISVILLE TIMES
COVINGTON TRUST & BANKING COMPANY
MR. AND MRS. GEORGE P. CROUNSE / GEORGE E. EVANS, JR.
FARMERS BANK & CAPITAL TRUST COMPANY / FISHER-PRICE TOYS, MURRAY
MARY PAULINE FOX, M.D., IN HONOR OF CHLOE GIFFORD
MARY A. HALL, M.D., IN HONOR OF PAT LEE,
JANICE HALL & MARY ANN FAULKNER
OSCAR HORNSBY INC. / OFFICE PRODUCTS DIVISION IBM CORPORATION
JERRY'S RESTAURANTS / ROBERT B. JEWELL
LEE S. JONES / KENTUCKIANA GIRL SCOUT COUNCIL
KENTUCKY BANKERS ASSOCIATION / KENTUCKY COAL ASSOCIATION, INC.
THE KENTUCKY JOCKEY CLUB, INC. / THE LEXINGTON WOMAN'S CLUB
LINCOLN INCOME LIFE INSURANCE COMPANY
LORILLARD A DIVISION OF LOEW'S THEATRES, INC.
METROPOLITAN WOMAN'S CLUB OF LEXINGTON / BETTY HAGGIN MOLLOY
MUTUAL FEDERAL SAVINGS & LOAN ASSOCIATION
NATIONAL INDUSTRIES, INC. / RAND MCNALLY & COMPANY
PHILIP MORRIS, INCORPORATED / MRS. VICTOR SAMS
SHELL OIL COMPANY, LOUISVILLE
SOUTH CENTRAL BELL TELEPHONE COMPANY
SOUTHERN BELLE DAIRY CO. INC.
STANDARD OIL COMPANY (KENTUCKY)
STANDARD PRINTING CO., H. M. KESSLER, PRESIDENT
STATE BANK & TRUST COMPANY, RICHMOND
THOMAS INDUSTRIES INC. / TIP TOP COAL CO., INC.
MARY L. WISS, M.D. / YOUNGER WOMAN'S CLUB OF ST. MATTHEWS

William Goebel

THE POLITICS OF WRATH

JAMES C. KLOTTER

THE UNIVERSITY PRESS OF KENTUCKY

Cover:
William Goebel campaigning in Owenton
Harper's Weekly

Frontispiece:
William Goebel speaking
at Bowling Green, 1899
Photo courtesy of the Kentucky Library,
Western Kentucky University

Research for The Kentucky Bicentennial Bookshelf
is assisted by a grant from the
National Endowment for the Humanities.
Views expressed in the Bookshelf do not
necessarily represent those of the Endowment.

ISBN: 0-8131-0240-5

Library of Congress Catalog Card Number: 77-76335

Copyright © 1977 by The University Press of Kentucky

A statewide cooperative scholarly publishing agency
serving Berea College, Centre College of Kentucky,
Eastern Kentucky University, The Filson Club,
Georgetown College, Kentucky Historical Society,
Kentucky State University, Morehead State University,
Murray State University, Northern Kentucky University,
Transylvania University, University of Kentucky,
University of Louisville, and Western Kentucky University.

Editorial and Sales Offices: Lexington, Kentucky 40506

To Karen, Christopher,
& Katherine

Contents

Preface

Misinformation about William Goebel abounds. The scarcity of published material is surprising concerning a man represented by historian C. Vann Woodward as the leader of "the first Southern reform movement to make a determined fight for power." Yet this same man so angered his opposition that his assassination finally occurred. Volumes have been written about other American assassinations—Lincoln, Garfield, McKinley, the Kennedys, and King. But, comparatively, very little scholarly work has been done on this single instance in our nation's history where a governor died in office as a result of assassination.

Obviously, this brief work is far from definitive. Nor does it exhaustively examine the assassination. Rather, it studies the public career of William Goebel, the atmosphere that resulted in his death, and his place in politics at a particularly crucial time for Kentucky and the nation. If this study stimulates further research, part of the author's objectives will be met. Newspaperman Urey Woodson once remarked, "Even in our own State the present generation has but a smattering knowledge of this period. That is what has impelled me to write this story." What he wrote in 1936 holds true four decades later, and so this book is an initial attempt to correct that situation.

For such a work, where no large collection of the subject's papers exists, many institutions must be visited in a search for material. In particular I wish to acknowledge the aid of William R. Buster, George M. Chinn, Hambleton Tapp, and many others at the Kentucky Historical Society; Jacqueline Bull and William J. Marshall of Special Collections at Margaret I. King Library, University of Kentucky; Nelson L.

Dawson and James R. Bentley of The Filson Club, Louisville; Edison H. Thomas of the Louisville and Nashville Railroad; and various members of the Kentucky Library at Western Kentucky University, the Lexington Public Library, the Library of Congress, the Cincinnati Law School, and Kenyon College.

To critical readers of the manuscript whose suggestions were what every writer should hope for—although I stubbornly did not follow them all—go my sincere thanks. Often stopping their own work to read the manuscript were John David Smith, Thomas H. Appleton, Jr., James Larry Hood, Gaye Keller Bland, all of Lexington; Norman L. Snider of Frankfort; and Charles G. Talbert of the University of Kentucky.

If I were only iconoclastic enough this preface would begin, rather than close, with acknowledgement of the aid of my typist, counselor, and wife. Freda is in reality coauthor of all my work, though her interest in history admittedly lags at times. To our children, who repeatedly ask "What's history?" we dedicate this work.

1

"LOOK UPON OPPOSITION AS OPPORTUNITY"

E ARLY ON TUESDAY morning, the sixth of February 1900, a train carrying the assassinated governor's body slowly moved from Cincinnati toward the station at Covington. Men, women, and children, old and young, friend and foe, lined the tracks to watch the train pass. Stores shut down and workers left their jobs. Thousands gathered at the station and silently watched the pallbearers lift out the casket. William Goebel was returning home.

As the procession moved toward the hall where the body would lie in state crowds grew so thick that police had to clear the way. Finally the cortege reached its destination and the casket was placed in the middle of a large room. A minister from Saint Paul's German Protestant Church offered a prayer in German, asking that God have mercy on the soul of the assassin. When the hall was opened to the public, the mass of the "common people" passed by; estimates of their numbers reached 100,000. When the casket was closed late that evening thousands more stood waiting outside.

In the darkness of an early morning rainstorm the next day the casket was brought back to the Queen and Crescent line train, which moved north toward Cincinnati, then south toward Frankfort. The direct route on the Louisville and Nashville tracks would not be taken—a final, bitter rebuff to the line which had so opposed the man now dead. As the train passed through northern Kentucky at every town and hamlet, every village and station, people stood in the rain for a final view of the dead leader. The train finally reached Frankfort and the casket was taken to the Capitol Hotel.

For four hours the next morning some 20,000 central Kentuckians paid their respects, despite the cloudburst which flooded the streets. In the afternoon the funeral procession moved up the hill toward the cemetery. Cold, fierce rain and wind made umbrellas useless. In the line of mourners that stretched for a quarter-mile, most were completely drenched. Yet they came.

After songs and prayers, former Senator J. C. S. Blackburn delivered the funeral oration. At one time the enemy of the dead man, he now spoke as a loving ally and ended by saying that the fallen leader, "lived an honest life and gave his life for your deliverance. Of him no eulogy, but truth may say, 'Earth never pillowed upon her bosom a truer son, nor heaven opened wide her portals to receive a manlier spirit.' " The people applauded as at a political rally. After a brief address by the new governor and a benediction, the funeral was concluded.

And so William Goebel became in death a martyr for the Democracy, a "folk hero" to his party, a man honored and remembered, a much-loved symbol. He became in death, then, something he never was in life.

For a man who received such political honors, William Goebel had not been a particularly appealing figure. Of medium height, he remained generally trim throughout his career. But most of his distinctive features that people remembered were not pleasant ones. They recalled the contemptuous lips; the sharp nose; the small, "ferret-like," glassy, dark-blue, humorless eyes; the black, slicked-down hair; the pale face; the heavy jaws. Author Irvin S. Cobb, who had followed Goebel as a young reporter, later wrote, "I never saw a man who, physically, so closely suggested the reptilian as this man did." Very little in Goebel's physical makeup added to his political attractiveness.

In death—and to a lesser degree in life—he symbolized the common man's friend. Yet the opponent analyzed well who saw Goebel as an autocrat, "but an autocrat not born to the purple." Had he been of a haughty, upper-class family of long social standing, Goebel's aloofness, his coolness toward "the people," would be less surprising. His simple life-style, his aid to the needy, even his sympathies reflect a surface commitment to the masses. Yet on a person-to-person basis, he was not one of them, nor could he be.

Apparently warm and rather witty in the company of friends, Goebel gave few observers this impression in public. He disliked mixing in crowds and remained cautious and aloof with those he did not know, "as though he were accustomed to spies." He belonged to few lodges or clubs. A reporter in one of Goebel's campaigns found a cold, secluded man who rarely shook hands "and never appears to seek popularity." He did not offer voters a ready smile and outstretched hand as he sought approval. Instead he gave them a taciturn and phlegmatic politician who appeared as a "synthetic, self-assembled mechanism."

Nor did Goebel become suddenly charismatic on the speaker's platform. Even among his friends few called him an orator, and he rarely excited great enthusiasm in his audience. By the standards of his time Goebel was not a good public speaker. He did not use the flowery images common in oratory, and when compared to usual addresses of the era, Goebel's speeches seem dry and imageless. This is not to say that they were ineffective. Goebel's deep, harsh voice carried well and he stated his points plainly and forcibly. He left his audience with little doubt about his position on an issue. When coupled to somewhat demagogic appeals and to an occasional phrase that stirred emotions, this delivery made for an effective speech, but never more than an average one.

Friend and foe alike agreed that Goebel's ambition relentlessly drove him onward without rest. A bold man in a fight, Goebel had strong desires and an inner drive to satisfy them. Little disturbed or discouraged him. A man of strong willpower, he would make a careful estimate of a situation and proceed slowly, methodically, and often successfully toward his goal. To achieve his aims required the use of power, and "he loved power," Cobb believed, "as drunkards love their bottle." Goebel sometimes submerged good motives in his search for authority, and it became increasingly difficult for him to perceive sincere opposition in others. Friends who honestly differed with him evolved—in his view—into enemies who had sold their souls to the devils he saw himself opposing. "Hate," an opponent noted, "could burn in him to a white heat, but he could not conceive that men would sacrifice a political career to a political principle."

To one friend Goebel had few qualities of a great politician, "save a great mind." Goebel's "great intellect" impressed figures on both sides of politics. Cobb, not a supporter, wrote some forty years after Goebel's death that he had not yet met a man whose mental ability so impressed him as Goebel's had. Prominent Kentuckians echoed those thoughts and stated that Goebel was the best-informed man they knew. Goebel did read widely, and many of his programs owed more to his knowledge of what other states had done than to any original thought. But his real strength lay not in his learning, but rather in his mental powers. He might make mistakes, even serious ones; but in a battle of intellects Goebel had the advantage.

When it came to the gathering of votes, however, Goebel's ability to organize served him better than his intellect. Many politicians of his era could operate behind the scenes, and then give a public appearance that their election had resulted from the massive, unbridled will of the people. Goebel found it difficult to project that public image. He had to rely almost solely on organization, and as a political organizer he had few peers.

Bold, arrogant, confident, tenacious, often having a political world to gain and little to lose, he could be absolutely fearless and extremely forceful in pursuing his goals. "This matter of achievement," he told a friend, "is more of the will than of the brain." As a contemporary noted, Goebel simply had "audacity, ruthlessness, a genius of leadership, an instinct for absolute despotism, a gift for organization, a perfect disregard for other men's rights . . . where his own wishes were concerned; the brain to plan and the will to execute."

Here, then, was a new and different type of Kentucky politician, one who was something of a paradox even to his few intimates. The private and public images of William Goebel did not always agree, and the contradictions in his life confused all but a few of those who knew him.

Controversy surrounded Goebel all his life and even obscured his origins. Opponents would claim that Goebel had been born in Europe, but they were mistaken. Nevertheless, his cultural roots and heritage did lie deeply buried in the soil of Germany. There revolutions had erupted in the 1840s and their failure had driven many Germans to seek better things in the New World. Among the mass of immigrants of the 1850s were the Goebels from Hannover. A young William Goebel (Sr.) had left the familiar but unstable and uncertain life of the old country for the unknown promise of the new. With the same wave of immigrants came a young woman, Augusta, also from Hannover.

Perhaps following relatives and friends to Pennsylvania, William and Augusta there started a new life together. They were married on 19 April 1855, according to a note in the family papers. While the new husband sought to make his carpentry and cabinetmaking trade a success, the wife worked in the log cabin they had built. And they prepared for their first child. According to a biographer who knew Goebel and his brothers, the child came two months prematurely. On 4 January 1856, in Sullivan County, Pennsylvania, a boy weighing less than three pounds was born. He was named Wilhelm Justus Goebel, but as the family adopted American ways he became simply William Goebel.

If he was premature, and Goebel had to struggle for survival from the very first, his birth may explain much of his adult life. For he would never stop fighting—first for his physical, later for his political, life. That he accomplished what he did in so short a time is less a tribute to the dream of the open society that may have brought his parents to America, than to Goebel's own strong, determined character, which was perhaps shaped by birth.

Less conjectural is the influence Goebel's mother had on his life. With the coming of the Civil War family responsibilities rested on her. Goebel's father, like many German immigrants in the East and Midwest, supported the Federal cause; and he was mustered into the service as a private. During those periods when her husband was away, Augusta Goebel reared a growing family virtually alone. A second son, Justus Jacob, had been born in 1858 and a daughter, Minia Augusta ("Minnie"), three years following that, on the eve of the war. Two years later, the third son and final child, Arthur William Goebel, was born.

As they matured all the children felt the lingering influence of their German background. William, for example, did not speak English until he was six years old, and his Old World heritage was stressed. Goebel's background and early life— something he could not influence or change—would later create uneasiness among Kentuckians. He was almost a foreigner, an interloper, only one generation away from Europe and its perceived evils. Goebel represented too much of the alien and unknown to many Kentuckians, some of whom had elected a nativist, Know-Nothing governor before the Civil War. Goebel's heritage would win him votes in the German community, but would weaken his appeal elsewhere.

Much of his early learning and the stress on his German roots came from the mother to whom William grew very devoted. One who knew both mother and son wrote later that Goebel "was singularly like his mother and from her he inherited . . . her marked individuality." A gentle, silent woman, she was the inspiration "that fired the spark of [his] ambition." Years after the war when she suffered a serious and painful illness and became an invalid, the one who cared for her with singular devotion was her firstborn. Augusta Goebel died on 16 July 1880, when William was twenty-four years old.

Though never a religious man, William Goebel kept her memory by paying the pew rent in the church she cherished. Seven years following her death, just before he entered politics, Goebel went for solitude to his mother's grave in Highland Cemetery. For there lay the remains of a force that lived on within him.

His father's return from war had brought the paternal influence back into Goebel's life. The destruction had not touched Sullivan County, and so it was some other motive that prompted the Goebels' move to Covington, Kentucky. The father apparently held different jobs there. At one time he operated a boardinghouse; at other times he owned a small store, worked in a saloon, and, in one account, labored as a railroad employee. If he did work for a railroad—the evidence is fragmentary—and he did experience disillusionment and harsh treatment, that might help to explain the son's later antipathy toward Kentucky railroads. It would have been easy for the younger Goebel to have vengeful feelings toward those who had wronged his father, even if Goebel himself did not recognize the emotions within. The father certainly did not rise far into the middle class, if even that far; the immigrant's son thus came from a plebeian background. When Goebel told of his common origins in later life, he spoke the truth: "I sold papers when my feet were almost on the ground. . . . I have stared poverty in the face and overcome it."

And overcome it he had, for by the time he uttered those words he had become one of the wealthiest lawyers in his section of the state. Obviously the road to the law was difficult for someone of Goebel's background. His father had wanted him to become a jeweler, and the young Goebel accordingly had become an apprentice in Duhme's jewelry store in Cincinnati. But he shortly was accepted as a student in a prominent law firm, where his rise began.

No more prominent lawyer practiced in Covington than the senior member of this firm. John White Stevenson by the mid-1870s had already served in the Kentucky legislature, in the 1849 constitutional convention, in Congress for two terms, as postwar lieutenant governor, and as governor. A distin-

7

guished son of a past Speaker of of the House of Representatives, Stevenson at the time was a United States senator. Later, in 1880, he chaired the Democratic National Convention; and four years following that he became president of the American Bar Association, just two years before his death.

Goebel gained the old senator's attention and respect. Eventually he became Stevenson's law partner and the executor (without bond) of Stevenson's large estate. With the senator supporting him, Goebel had a powerful ally who introduced him to the inner circles of politics and law. And if Stevenson's powerful support was not enough, young Goebel soon gained the goodwill of an equally important Covington leader. A student of Stevenson's himself, John G. Carlisle in some ways surpassed his teacher. When Goebel became his law partner—probably on Stevenson's recommendation—Carlisle's career was ascendant. Coolly aloof yet hospitable, he traditionally wore black, which symbolically represented his somber mind. A man of forceful presence and impressive physique, Carlisle did not so much generate enthusiasm as respect.

For several years Goebel remained as his junior partner and when Carlisle became Speaker of the United States House of Representatives in 1883, the firm of Carlisle, Goebel, and Carlisle, at 11 Boone Block, was a prosperous one. In 1890, legislators selected Goebel's benefactor as senator and three years later Grover Cleveland chose him to be secretary of the treasury. By that time Goebel and Carlisle had parted; but Carlisle's friendship, like Stevenson's, better enabled William Goebel to achieve what he sought.

Though politics eventually became Goebel's chief love, his initial devotion went to the law. For he was an excellent attorney. His arguments and speeches showed a thorough knowledge of legal precedent and current interpretations. He knew his cases, his abilities, and his law. Goebel specialized in corporate and railroad cases, and in later years he proudly boasted that of his many lawsuits against the Louisville and Nashville line (the L & N) no jury returned a verdict unfavorable to his clients. In one such recorded case, a Kenton County woman engaged his services to recover damages from a wreck in which a relative had died. Since he could not get the entire amount she sought, Goebel said that it was "but fair that you should pay me one third of the amount recovered [though] our contract was for one half." He eventually received $1,511 and sent her $1,100 of the total. In gratitude she named her baby for him.

As this and other cases indicate, being a "railroad lawyer" could prove very rewarding financially. Representing Campbell and Kenton counties against the Central Bridge Company, for example, Goebel received one-third of the $150,000 the counties gained through his efforts. By 1899 his annual income approached $25,000. Although Goebel reportedly took some cases from laborers without a fee, in many others he obviously did quite well. Opponents would charge later that his contracts could be among "the keenest, cruelest known," and that he exploited rather than befriended the poor. That was a gross exaggeration. Still, Goebel did profit from his specialty. And a reputation as a poor man's lawyer would not hurt at election time.

By the time he entered politics, Goebel lived a plain, unexciting private life. He seldom visited the theater or indicated any interest in sports; he drank beer in moderation, and he quit smoking cigars in later life. "Timid and awkward in ladies' society," Goebel very seldom, if ever, was romantically linked to any woman. His life centered on his work. He usually retired to a little room with sparse furnishings—a split reed chair, a few pictures, a bed and a dresser, two ten-pound dumbbells and, of course, his books. When not involved in political rallies and the like, he spent his evenings reading and preparing for the political career he soon would begin. His creed, almost his motto for the coming years, lay in the words he wrote his brother when Arthur complained about the difficulty of studying the historian Herodotus. He should increase his efforts, advised William. He should—as William Goebel certainly did—follow the advice he had once heard: "Look upon opposition as opportunity."

2

REBELS,
REACTIONARIES,
AND REFORMERS

O<small>N</small> 30 D<small>ECEMBER</small> 1887, William Goebel took the oath required of a new state senator. With that he formally entered the political world he had long observed and had long prepared for, a world whose immediate origins went back to the Civil War. By the beginning of that war the Democratic party ruled from an unexpected position of prominence in the commonwealth. Kentucky was once a Whig stronghold and a virtual fiefdom of Henry Clay. But Clay's death in 1852 and his party's decline soon after had left Kentucky politics in disarray. A strong but short-lived, nativist, Know-Nothing movement had gathered enough strength to elect a governor in 1855, but the violence the party attracted—in addition to other factors—hastened its decline. As the war approached in 1861 only a loosely organized group called the "Opposition" contested the Democratic party. Almost by default, the Democracy had triumphed.

The war disrupted that brief ascendancy. By most indications, such as newspaper sentiment and army enlistments, the state favored the Union so loved by Clay and his successor in spirit, John J. Crittenden. By late 1862, the Union held Kentucky firmly. But events moved the state away from the Federal cause, and more and more citizens turned sympathetic eyes southward. After 1862 the Confederates made no serious threats to retake Kentucky, and so the excesses that accompany military rule were blamed solely on the Union side. In addition, Confederates who did enter the state after 1862, chiefly John Hunt Morgan's raiders, presented a dashing, heroic front to the populace. Though only partly the truth, such an image contrasted with that of the Union leaders who had the unfortunate responsibility of dealing with citizens day by day and facing problems Morgan's men never did. The southern cavalier became more and more attractive. Military interference in elections added to the mounting Federal problems.

Moreover, slaves were leaving the farms. After the first years Federal forces gave little indication that they would return them. The Emancipation Proclamation did not directly affect the state, but news of that event created unrest among slaves and angry resentment among state leaders. Even devoted Unionists openly questioned and criticized administration policy. Enrolling and then enlisting of slaves in the Union army—in return for their freedom and their family's—drove Union slaveholders (and there were many) headlong into the ranks of the political opposition. In an attempt to stop that movement, leaders of what would become the Republican party made more blunders. Whether correctly or not, they became identified in the popular mind with military rule and black emancipation. By 1864 the state had turned antiadministration and probably even prosouthern in sympathy. Soon after hostilities ended, a newspaper reported that Kentucky had waited until after the war to secede. In a much quoted remark, Lincoln had said that to lose Kentucky "is nearly the same as to lose the whole game." Although the Union did secure the commonwealth, the methods used to insure that victory shaped Kentucky politics for three decades.

William Goebel came to Covington after the Civil War and beheld a confused political state. This son of a Union veteran saw little indication that the victors in war were triumphing in peace. Although Republicans sought to build their party on a Union base, their hopes for dominance faded. Besides wartime images that had to be overcome, now the national Radical Republicans' policies alienated Kentuckians further. State Republicans tried to turn attention away from Reconstruction in the South, but the amalgamated group calling themselves Democrats capitalized on national affairs—to the consternation of the Republicans. Both groups sought to lure wandering ex-Whigs to their banner. Most, however, probably turned to the Democrats—particularly former slaveholders and southern sympathizers. Excesses that some saw in the Republican administration drove both ex-Whigs and former Union Democrats to the changing Democracy. A new and even more powerful coalition formed.

Republicans, in turn, sought to capitalize on old Whig animosities toward Democrats and on Union veterans' opposition to Confederates. In the main they failed. Kentuckians' amity for the South made the national Republican party's seeming excesses there more disagreeable. Kentucky Republicans had to settle for the role of minority party for three decades following 1865. Nevertheless strong Republican leaders arose—John Marshall Harlan, later a Supreme Court justice; Benjamin Helm Bristow, U. S. Grant's able secretary of the treasury; and, later, William O'Connell Bradley, the state's first Republican governor. Under these leaders the Republican party in Kentucky over the next thirty years not only garnered a sizable vote (as in other southern states), but also increased their vote as the years passed (unlike southern Republicans generally). By the time Goebel entered politics, Republican opposition had developed into a very formidable force, although one still trying to break free of the wartime memories that shackled it.

It was the Democrats, however, who controlled the state. And that control, for the most part, was in the hands of ex-Confederates or Confederate sympathizers. Humorist Petroleum V. Nasby (David Ross Locke) exaggerated but pinpointed the issue when he wrote in 1867 that "Ef no Confedrits wuz allowed to vote in Tennessee, thank the Lord no other kind wuz permitted to hist in ballots in Kentucky." He added that "here Dimocrasy kin flourish, ef nowhere else." The vast majority of Kentuckians who fought had done so for the Union, but the majority of Democrats who held major office after the war had served or supported the Confederacy. As a letter writer complained sometime later in the century, "It is a well established custom in Kentucky, that worthy and capable ex-confederate soldiers (especially if maimed) asking office of the people, are invariably thus 'pensioned.' " Goebel's Union ties would make it difficult for him to advance in postwar Democratic politics.

Although Democrats and ex-Confederates controlled the state, they were not in complete harmony. Factionalism divided the party. The twentieth-century saying that Kentucky Democrats would rather defeat each other than the Republicans was already proving accurate in the late nineteenth century. For a party whose diverse base rested on groups with strong feelings—ex-Whigs, ex-Unionists, and some ex-Know-Nothings—such differences would not be unexpected. Exacerbated by postwar problems, the differences surfaced and solidified.

But both factions agreed on several vital issues, and they usually united at election time. Both the Bourbon and New Departure Democrats decried the Reconstruction of the southern states, opposed centralization in government, and supported states rights. While the New Departure faction did favor governmental aid to railroads, for example, they—like the Bourbons—agreed that a general policy of laissez-faire was best. Thus when the inflammatory issue of blacks' rights faded with the gradual acceptance of the constitutional amendments, differences lessened. Other issues divided the factions, but by the early 1870s their most basic disagreements had ceased. The two terms—Bourbon and New Departure—soon came to mean about the same thing, and the Kentucky Democracy began to adhere to the overall southern pattern more closely.

Almost as soon as Bourbon-New Departure differences lessened in the early 1870s, the previously ignored voice of the disgruntled agrarian spoke out. Agrarian anger grew out of concentration in the postwar era on "this new mania of tobacco." Increasing cultivation of tobacco instead of varied crops made farmers more dependent on a single price. In the year before the Panic of 1873 tobacco prices reached ten cents; six years later they had fallen to half that figure. Laborers' wages decreased. A people in growing economic distress turned to quick answers and sought scapegoats. Railroads seemed appropriate villains. While the depression hit farmers hard, railroads prospered; their Kentucky mileage increased 50 percent between 1870 and 1880. Local communities went into long-term bonded indebtedness to finance and attract lines to their locales. Special taxation favored railroads and, while farmers lost property because they could not pay taxes on it, railroads often escaped even basic taxation.

The very agrarian ideal seemed under attack. A new ethos had challenged that ideal—and seemed to be winning. The age of railroads was coming to America, and to Kentucky. And while many praised the mobility, the expanded markets, and other advantages that this age brought, some—especially in economically difficult situations—saw only dangers. Still others believed in the railroads as potential forces for good, but supported stringent regulation of the powerful lines. All these groups, each with their own spokesmen, operated throughout Goebel's lifetime. Like agrarians, Goebel saw in railroad regulation a solution to many of the state's problems.

In the depression years of the 1870s agrarian anger focused on the railroads, but that problem required a long-range approach and promised little sudden success. To troubled farmers inflation and cheap money provided quicker answers to their ills. When the dominant Democrats did not encourage their demands, a third party rose from their ranks. The Greenback party, sometimes fusing with the minority Republicans, proved a potent, if uncertain, political force. A Murray resident wrote to future Senator William Lindsay in 1877 that his whole area was affected with "Grangerism, Greenbackism and Soreheadism."

Although the normally nonpolitical granges supported a

program similar to the Greenback party's, the two did not formally join forces. Nevertheless, in economically depressed western Kentucky the new party found quick acceptance. Here would be the center of Greenback strength, then later of the Populists, and then of Night Rider activity in the twentieth century. In the 1870s Democratic supremacy in the area was challenged, and Greenbackers gained close to a fifth of the vote in most counties. Statewide, the party's candidate for governor received over 8 percent of the vote in 1879. The decrease came in the Democratic margin.

Better times and Democratic acceptance of their rhetoric if not their programs returned agrarians to the Democracy. But in the granges, in the Farmers' Alliance later, and in the agrarians as a whole, a strong, silent force lay as if asleep. Economic conditions had turned voters away from their past partisanship. If new issues arose, if times again grew bad, if Democrats ignored their will, the agrarians were ready to rise up once more to threaten the party's hegemony. In the process, the old factional leaders might fall before a new order. Goebel sought to make certain that he would not be excluded from that agrarian future, should it come about.

Goebel, however, was not completely an agrarian, nor was he later, as some historians have suggested, a Populist. He did support many agrarian-Populist programs, and on many issues he stood on the same side politically. But the programs Goebel advocated that did coincide with agrarian ones, such as railroad regulation, grew out of a nonagrarian background, his urban experience. Other common causes were simply ones whose attainment had been long overdue in the state, and which now had gained wide popular appeal. Goebel was far from being "the First New Dealer" that a biographer called him, but he was closer in some ways to the urban Progressives of the twentieth century than to the Populists of the nineteenth.

When Kentucky agrarians in the 1870s and 1880s, and later the Populists, appealed—with only limited success—to the urban laborer, then Goebel and the agrarians moved nearest to each other in their programs. For Goebel's real base was the urban working class. Out of that class had come his family. Goebel's entire adult life had been spent in Covington, then Kentucky's second largest city. He had handled workmen's cases, and—whether by design or by chance—had won much support from them. His stands on many issues, such as railroad regulation, were based on his dealings in an urban framework. As Kentucky almost matched the tremendous pace of industrialization in the nation between 1865 and 1900, urban groups grew in potential importance. Although labor unions in the commonwealth, as elsewhere, struggled unsuccessfully to gain large numbers of adherents, they did win some victories and gain some strength, particularly in Louisville and northern Kentucky. The significance of that force was not lost on an ambitious politician like Goebel.

In election year 1887, the signs were unmistakable. That year the union labor movement peaked in nineteenth-century Kentucky. At first glance such would seem to favor candidate Goebel, who sought his first political office. With state Senator James W. Bryan as the Democratic nominee for lieutenant governor, his seat and the remainder of his term was vacated. Backed by the powerful Carlisle and former allies of Stevenson, Goebel was expected to win the election easily.

But workers dissatisfied with the Democratic party's continued conservatism and resistance to change organized a third party—as the Greenbackers had only eight years before. The Union Labor party developed no strength outside of cities, and little overall except in northern Kentucky. While separate at the state level, the Republicans and Union Labor forces occasionally united locally.

In Kenton County the Union Labor party did fuse to oppose the Democrats and William Goebel. And not surprisingly. For while Goebel actually could have supported the Union Labor party and most of its programs in some ways better than the state Democratic ones, he was very much a party man. He had allies in the Democracy, and if he deserted them or alienated them by supporting Union Labor stands, his political future might be ended. A new party, no matter how powerful, was too uncertain an entity to gain the support of an ambitious politician with strong party backing.

There was no question that Goebel faced a difficult foe in the fused Union Labor forces. Although he might stress his past actions for laborers and his working-class origins, Goebel had to recognize that his former mentor Stevenson had been the chief counsel for the Kentucky Central Railroad and other large corporations, and thus was an enemy of the Union Labor party. His past association with Stevenson might help Goebel in certain circles of the Democratic party, but in others it would cost him votes. Goebel had other handicaps as well. He was a political novice, he had no record to support his rhetoric, and he was not a good stump speaker. Yet most analysts did not foresee a large Union Labor vote. As usual the Democrats—and Goebel—should win.

The August election returns indicated widespread dissatisfaction with the Democratic party. On the state level, popular ex-Confederate General Simon B. Buckner won his gubernatorial race by the smallest margin since the war's end. The Republicans had now shown that with a clever campaigner, such as "Billy O. B." Bradley, they could threaten seriously. Wartime memories still faded slowly, however.

While the Union Labor party received less than 2 percent of the state vote overall, in northern Kentucky the results were far different. The party carried neighboring Campbell County (Newport) over both Democrats and Republicans; among the three state representatives selected in Kenton County was one Union Labor man. Only exceptional Democrats survived the labor onslaught.

In the Twenty-Fourth Senatorial District the race was too close to call. Initial reports indicated that the Union Labor fusion candidate (a former Republican) had beaten the Democratic nominee, William Goebel, by over one hundred votes. "Quite contrary to Democratic expectations," urban areas of the district gave a Union Labor majority. When the official tally was announced, Goebel had won, as expected, but by a margin of only fifty-six votes.

In two years, at the expiration of Bryan's original senate term, Goebel would have to face reelection. Given the unexpected closeness of his victory, he had to ensure that dissatisfied working-class Democrats would return to the party and vote for him or his career would end. Clearly even his faint association with corporations (through Stevenson) would have to be overcome—the political climate so dictated. Goebel needed to impress alienated laborers that he opposed the same things they did. Otherwise reelection might never come. But if he could become the spokesman for the disgruntled electorate, then his political possibilities were more promising. Ambition dictated one future course for William Goebel.

3

GOEBEL
AND THE GOVERNORS

THE POLITICAL WORLD William Goebel entered in December 1887 was rapidly changing, as he had quickly discovered in his campaign. Old alliances faded as quickly as new ones were made. In this quicksand of transitional politics, Goebel faced the added burden of being basically a northerner in a state that thought itself southern. His past political allies had gotten him to the state senate, but one short session did not afford much time to rise above the commonplace. Consequently, in the legislature the freshman senator from Kenton sought and commanded notice quickly. He did so by following the old dictum that if you want to attract attention, denounce the largest, easiest target available. The Louisville and Nashville Railroad would prove a formidable foe, however. Its wealth had increased phenomenally following the war. In 1870 the L & N had declared a dividend of 40 percent; a decade later the dividend was 100 percent. Louisville and towns along the line gave generously in financial aid and political support. As the L & N expanded its influence southward beyond state lines it made the Falls City a center of southern trade. In Henry Watterson's words, Louisville's "union of pork, tobacco and whiskey will make us all wealthy, healthy and frisky."

Between 1865 and 1880 total railroad mileage in the state trebled, and these lines introduced Kentucky's rural areas to a more exciting, vibrant way of life. But at the same time excesses biased people's views of the progress. For with railroads came discriminatory rates and other measures that angered small farmers in particular. The resulting Greenback discontent of the 1870s culminated in the creation in 1880 of a weak state Railroad Commission. Under the leadership of candid, self-assured, energetic, ruthless Milton Hannibal Smith, the L & N struck back at this step in what it saw as an organized attempt to cripple or destroy the line. Smith later explained his thoughts on any legislature's actions when he told the Interstate Commerce Commission that "all legislative bodies are a menace." To control this "menace" a strong, active, and well-funded lobby was organized in Frankfort. Largely guided by John Hunt Morgan's former chief lieutenant and brother-in-law, talented little Basil Duke, the lobby became so powerful that one writer moaned "a man could not be elected justice of the peace or school trustee without the sanction of the Louisville and Nashville politicians."

The L & N contributed sums of money to politicians who supported it faithfully, and it retained large numbers of lawyers throughout the state on its payroll. Many became legislators. Free travel passes were distributed widely to officeholders and politicians for reasons not difficult to ascertain: a judge should receive a pass, as he was a "very valuable aid to us"; a black pastor, for he is a "pretty influential man amongst his people"; another judge, because "we are liable to have to call on him for help at almost any time." Favored friends and political allies could travel courtesy of the L & N on any line within the state or the South. In such ways, supporting the L & N could be made very attractive for a politician. But not for William Goebel. Up until 1887 few politicans had dared to oppose the L & N line. Newspapers, such as Henry Watterson's *Courier-Journal*, promoted its efforts. Within five years after creation of the Railroad Commission, Duke's railroad lobby had done its work well. In 1884 the legislature granted a five-year tax exemption to any newly constructed lines. The governor—a man Goebel had supported— let the law go into effect without his signature. By the end of that decade a quarter of the state's roads would be free of taxation. The railroad lobby grew more powerful and, to its opponents, more dangerous. The Railroad Commission reported that it had become a regular policy now to keep a paid lobby in Frankfort, "to interfere with the Legislature." A Republican paper commented that support of the lobby was necessary before any prominent measure could be passed. This was the situation at the end of 1887, when Governor Buckner recommended increasing the powers of the Railroad Commission and discontinuing exemptions to railroad property.

Shocked at Buckner's actions, the railroads countered with a bill that in effect would abolish the commission. The governor's recommendation for increased powers got nowhere, as allies had to fight even to keep the commission in existence. Free passes, meals, drinks, and other luxuries were distributed lavishly by the lobby. The bill passed the house by a 46-26 vote. In the interim, however, a committee was set up to investigate the lobby's actions. William Goebel was selected to represent the senate and by the time he finished his task he had few, if any, doubts of the correctness of his position regarding railroads. After hearing testimony the five-man committee presented its findings. Goebel personally drafted and introduced the report, which denounced the lobby, but recommended only a grand jury investigation. The committee found a "large and influential" lobby at work, entertaining members and furnishing "whiskey & c." Although there was a well-planned "and extraordinarily powerful effort to dominate the Legislature," the investigators found no evidence that money or anything of value had been given to influence votes. The senate rejected the bill to abolish the commission, however.

Goebel came out of the lobby investigation convinced that the L & N's powers needed curbing. Condemnation of the evils of the lobby became frequent in his rhetoric. Goebel had found an issue that he would never let go of. The response to his efforts showed what popularity attacks on monopolies could have. The age of corporate restriction slowly was coming to Kentucky, and Goebel moved comfortably in the mainstream, if not the forefront.

Not all of Goebel's attentions focused on the one issue of railroad regulation, however. Several of the bills the young legislator introduced showed his concern for laborers—or, as his detractors would argue, at least a concern for their votes. Goebel's very first move was to offer a bill to repeal a minor 1886 turnpike law protecting turnpikes in which the state had an interest. Poorer people found the high tolls and monopolistic controls involved in these improved roads unacceptable during difficult financial times. There was a growing effort to make these roads "free," and by 1888 lawless force was being used when persuasion failed. In the 1890s this lawlessness grew—and eventually it achieved its object. Goebel early proclaimed his sympathies, and when violence later erupted his stand placed him—to conservatives' eyes—on the side of the lawless who sought to take property (toll roads) without compensation. Goebel introduced a few other bills that concerned railroads and corporations, but in the main the session was a learning experience, as is usually the case for newcomers to the General Assembly. Events were more instructive than usual, however, and they strengthened Goebel's growing inclination to view Bourbon-New Departure Democracy with disdain.

The most unsettling revelation came about unexpectedly. Republicans and a small number of Democrats pushed for an examination of the treasurer's office. Finally the legislature reluctantly agreed. James W. Tate, the incumbent treasurer, had served since 1868, and his popularity was surpassed by few state politicians. Opponents found it difficult to convince his many friends in the legislature that there could even be a hint of scandal associated with "Honest Dick" Tate. Then, on 20 March 1888, Governor Buckner's message announced to a startled General Assembly that the treasurer had been missing for several days. A shortage of public funds had been discovered. Wild rumors spread, and politicians came under sudden and close public scrutiny. The auditor of the state, another perennial officeholder, was blamed for not examining state accounts more closely. Other politicians, including former Governor Preston Leslie, had accepted loans from Tate—loans that now seemed certain to have come from treasury funds. These men—like others—had trusted the friendly, kind, and accommodating Tate. Now their political careers were threatened by that association.

Tate's defalcations were eventually shown to have totalled some $247,000. The whereabouts of "Honest Dick" himself remained a mystery. Dick Tate and the state's money both had disappeared, never to be heard from again. In Frankfort the public outcry threatened to disrupt Bourbon-New Departure ascendancy. Tate's case was not exceptional in the Democratic South at the time, as some Republicans gleefully noted. To calm their critics, the legislature created the office of State Examiner to prevent any repetition of the Tate affair. Impeachment proceedings began in the senate on 30 March 1888. Goebel, along with almost the entire senate, voted Tate guilty of each article. Removal of Tate and tardy remedial legislation did not end the suspicion and clamor. Public distrust of elected officials continued. When the Court of Appeals declared that Tate's wealthy bondsmen—prominent party leaders—would not be held liable for his defalcations, anger increased. Eventually the whole episode influenced the 1890–91 constitutional convention's decision to limit officeholders to one term, to ensure that no future Dick Tate could rule his domain unchecked.

Goebel, a newcomer, had remained untouched by the scandal, and in many ways he profited from it. One of a new and younger breed of politicians who sought to challenge established party leaders, the Kenton County senator had fresh ammunition for his onslaught, and also new allies. Rising discontent with the old order, and Goebel's successful efforts to disengage himself from that group, made his future much more promising than when the session had begun.

Reelection now faced the incumbent. Goebel did not have the oratorical powers and personal charisma so useful in campaigns, but he did have the ability—however imperfect—to articulate the long-suppressed but now surfacing discontent felt by agrarians and urban laborers. His ideas were generally not original, and were based on his knowledge of developments in other states. But to voters the source meant little. Goebel spoke and, more importantly, acted for them. They saw in him a voice for reform. He had accomplished what he sought and he had projected, in modern terminology, a favorable image.

Goebel returned to Covington with a reputation that gave him significant mass popularity. The ex-Union Labor supporters posed no threat now, and Goebel usually could count on Covington's large and influential German vote. In the 1889 senatorial race Goebel, running without opposition, won a new term, despite a still unsettled situation. Four years later Goebel outpolled his Republican opponent by a three-to-one margin, the largest majority in the county. By that time Goebel had secured a strong base from which to operate.

If there has been a single crucial decade in Kentucky's political history, it was the 1890s. Goebel's dominant Democratic party entered the decade totally supreme, having averaged 61 percent of the gubernatorial vote over the past quarter-century. Divided by factionalism but united for the most part at election time, the Democracy wielded great national influence and almost total control in a majority of Kentucky counties. But as the 1890s came to an end, Republicans constantly, and often successfully, challenged Democrats. In the three decades following 1900 a near division of the office of governor would result, with four Democrats winning that office, versus three Republicans. The factionalism present at the start of the 1890s developed into full-blown rebellion, and political alliances of major import were transformed. Not until the upheavals brought about by the New Deal would another such division occur.

What had happened? For one thing, familar economic stresses again operated. Falling farm prices—tobacco declined to 3.7 cents in 1896—coupled with laborers' problems following the 1893 depression, brought agrarian and urban discontent to the surface. Angry workers in farm and factory struck out at the enemies they thought they saw in financial and corporate monopolies. Once again, men and women desperate for answers to their despair turned to panaceas. In Kentucky they vented their anger on toll roads and railroads, and in the state, as elsewhere, they began to cry out for the inflationary scheme represented in free silver. Two decades of basically static rule in the commonwealth, and memories of the Tate affair, made current leadership unacceptable.

To compound the problems, prevalent political theory could not meet the challenges without major modifications. When none came, more stress resulted—and more discontent. Forces opposing change threatened to bring about their own defeat by resisting needed reforms. President Grover Cleveland's earlier veto message on a bill to provide farmers needed grass seed—government's functions "do not include the support of the people"—would not satisfy the temper of the 1890s. Above all and for whatever reason the world was changing rapidly, and the political philosophy of Grover Cleveland contrasted sharply, as if it belonged to another time, with that of Theodore Roosevelt. The beginning of the new century symbolized more than entry into another hundred year period: twentieth-century Kentuckians would live in an era far different from that of only a decade before. Events and changing currents of opinion brought about this transformation, but so did individuals. There were giants on the national, regional, and state scenes—some of noble cast, others of lesser quality. One of these men—and observers bitterly disagreed over which group he belonged to—greatly influenced the decade of the 1890s. But William Goebel did not long survive it.

The decade began with a gubernatorial campaign that showed the diversity of sectional, economic, and class feelings operating in Kentucky. And a new third party once more threatened Democratic control. While the generally non-political Farmers' Alliance had preferred to work for their demands through major parties, they did indicate willingness to enter the political arena should circumstances warrant. Some members became convinced that some formal, organized effort should be made. And so on 20 May 1891 a group of seventy men who were attending the Cincinnati national convention of the Populists crossed the Ohio and organized the People's party of Kentucky. Former Greenbackers took the initial leadership posts.

Democrats recognized the threat posed, especially in the troubled flatlands of western Kentucky. "Warnings" there admitted that "there is an unrest in the minds and feelings of many" who are usually Democrats. "This element," a writer continued, "chiefly farmers, are honestly impatient as to existing grievances." Although handicapped by mediocre leadership and the stigma of Republican collaboration, the Populists gained a respectable vote that August. The totals matched the averages of earlier third parties and indicated the resentment felt toward both major parties. The 25,000 votes represented less than 9 percent of the vote, but given the Republicans' rising strength, this percentage became more crucial than in earlier races.

More so than in the formal People's party vote, however, the agrarian influence was felt in the Democratic party. Alliance men endorsed as Democrats made up half of the legislators elected to the house. And while party man Goebel had no use for people who took votes from his Democracy, he did recognize agrarian strength in his party and he appealed to it.

Alliance and Populist strength permeated the constitutional convention of 1890–91 as well. Kentucky's fourth—and present—constitution was framed by politicians aware of and influenced by agrarians. Goebel felt these pressures, but an analysis of his role indicates that—once again—his interest was in urban, not rural, matters. He and the Populist spokesmen often found themselves on opposite sides of issues. Except when it came to railroads and corporations. Goebel's reputation and past actions had resulted in a strong attempt by the railroads to prevent his selection for the convention. They had failed. On 8 September 1890 Goebel and other delegates assembled; final adjournment did not come until twelve months later.

During that time Goebel sat in distinguished company. Former Governor Proctor Knott and present Governor Buckner represented the old Bourbon-New Departure Democrats; Populist leader Thomas Pettit—"Little War Cloud"—ably served his party; and future gubernatorial hopeful Dr. J. D. Clardy watched Alliance interests. An independent reformer such as Winchester's W. M. Beckner influenced many convention matters. Very slender, quite bald—like "a skinned onion on a bean pole"—so sour-looking that newspapermen called him "Rain-in-the-face," he served on more committees than anyone and helped shape many reform measures. The thirty-six-year-old Goebel had able and experienced allies and enemies.

Somewhat surprisingly, Goebel played only a minor role in the debates, although he would exaggerate that role as the years passed. Part of his lack of influence simply resulted from frequent absences: of the 250 days of the sessions he was present for only 100, according to one study. A random sample of nonadjournment roll-call votes gives the same figure: Goebel voted on only two of every five roll calls on the average. This record resulted partly from his duties in the senate, which at times was in session while the convention met; but it also probably came from sheer boredom, for convention debates grew tedious and repetitious. Still, for such an important document, Goebel gave little of his time.

The Kenton County delegate had called for a flexible document that would allow legislatures to pass laws as future needs arose. The resultant document was just the opposite; agrarians did not trust the future. Even Goebel's own actions tended to produce effects contrary to his stated desires. One issue did bring Goebel to the debates and elicited his strongest efforts. Railroad regulation continued to be his consuming theme, and his rhetoric on that issue read well to voters. Goebel explained that he sought to prevent anything in the constitution from "being used by the railroad corporations to evade their just

proportion of the burden of taxation." In defense of a clause
that dealt with recovering railroad damages from employees,
Goebel insisted that "paid lobbyists" had kept legislative bills
on this subject from coming to a vote. This "existing evil"
should be corrected by the constitution. The section was incorporated.

In practice then, Goebel used the constitution as a vehicle
to enact laws which he had not been able to pass in the more
conservative legislature. Although he spoke for flexibility,
when it came to certain issues he voted for specificity. This
was particularly true of his chief aim—incorporation of the
Railroad Commission into the new document, which would
make it a constitutional office above the powers of the lobby.
On that issue he prevailed. The unwieldy constitution eventually included specific sections controlling rebates, drawbacks,
discriminatory freight rates, and preferential contracts. While
the railroad issue dominated Goebel's debates when he appeared at sessions, he occasionally supported other measures.
He spoke out—unsuccessfully—against poll taxes; and he attempted to win a board of labor arbitration with compulsory
powers, which the constitution did make a future possibility.
Two sections he strongly advocated were successfully incorporated: power to set a minimum age for working children, and
worker payment in currency rather than company store
checks.

Despite strong opposition from the L & N and from the
Courier-Journal ("It is an Alliance Constitution," Henry Watterson sneered), the document won widespread voter approval. More a legislative enactment than a flexible constitution, it became quickly outdated, though not in Goebel's
lifetime. He had reason to be proud, for he had helped to
secure the Railroad Commission's permanency; and he had
worked—if not hard—for several other needed reforms. His
political standing rose.

But actions by the governor elected in 1891 temporarily
slowed Goebel's ascendancy. John Young Brown, a member of
a prominent family, was in his fifties. He had been in political
life since his 1859 election to the United States Congress even

before he had reached the required age. Representing western Kentucky in the preconvention period, Brown capitalized on feelings in that area that it was their turn to have a gubernatorial nominee, as the Bluegrass had dominated the field since the war. Goebel worked hard for the nomination of his strong ally Cassius M. Clay. Nephew of his old emancipationist namesake, the wealthy Bourbon County farmer and president of the constitutional convention—like all candidates—desperately sought Alliance support. But that went elsewhere. Brown won the nomination and defeated a weak Republican candidate in the fall.

Goebel's differences with Brown did not heal easily. The new governor's course did not please either his Alliance supporters or Goebel. "I have fought him as hard as I could," the Kenton County senator wrote Clay. Brown responded by vetoing Goebel's local bills and by having the *Courier-Journal* attack the stands of the senator. In September 1892 Goebel accused Brown of relentlessly using "every means at his command to increase his power and patronage."

Goebel's alienation from Brown helped him win over disenchanted Alliance legislators, and his dealings in the constitutional convention had gained him new support. He still had the backing of prominent established party leaders, such as Clay and Carlisle. His 1894 selection as president pro tem of the senate, by a strict 25-11 party vote, thus came as no surprise. Goebel was developing into a formidable politician, and he did not let the governor's opposition slow his efforts.

At the same time depression deepened in Kentucky, and voter unrest grew with economic distress. In Louisville over forty businesses failed in 1893, and an estimated 10,000 unemployed workers sought simple livelihood. When the L & N reacted to falling business by cutting wages some 10 percent, over 1,400 workers united in protest. Other urban centers, especially along the Ohio River, joined the Pullman and other strikers. Goebel presented to the senate petitions of unemployed laborers and of unions; and, according to some reports, he defended without charge workers involved in strikes. These acts aided his reputation as the laborers' friend.

What the economic situation meant for the Democrats would be discovered in 1895. Clay again sought the gubernatorial nomination, over P. "Wat" Hardin. The money issue, unimportant four years earlier, now became crucial. A cheap money expedient, free silver, allowed debtors to pay debts more easily, but entrapped them later in inflationary prices for the goods they had to buy. Nevertheless, the immediate appeal outweighed the potential results. Many prominent Bourbon-New Departure leaders refused to support any free silver idea in 1895. Watterson, W. C. P. Breckinridge, Clay, Carlisle—now secretary of the treasury—all united in opposition and got a gold plank at the 1895 convention. Hardin's reputed alliance with railroad interests gained him some support from them. Goebel's choice, Clay, stood for gold and railroad regulation, and the senator supported him on both. But again Clay failed to receive the necessary votes, and Hardin won.

Sensing victory at last, the Republicans nominated their best campaigner, veteran W. O. Bradley. Stressing his "sound-money" stands, Bradley badgered Hardin to state his own views. Finally, in a disastrous joint debate in Louisville, Hardin came out for free silver. The gold plank he stood on fell apart. Many "Gold Bugs" deserted the party for Bradley, or simply did not vote. Although Hardin may have retained some silverites by his stand, others still went to the Populist candidate, Tom Pettit.

An already disunited Democracy divided on another issue, one that potentially threatened Goebel's future as well. The American Protective Association (A.P.A.) sought to defend "Americanism" against "foreign" social, religious, and political influences. "The rejuvenated ghost of Know-Nothingism," the A.P.A. directed its opposition toward Catholics and immigrants; in 1894 it had influenced the vote that defeated an Irish Catholic for Congress. Although members of both parties made up A.P.A. membership, in 1895 the organization worked for Bradley's election. The Republican candidate himself did not voice A.P.A. sentiments, but he accepted their votes. The next year the A.P.A. state president was rewarded by President William McKinley with the post of collector of internal revenue for Louisville. After 1896 the organization would not play an important role in elections, but the events of 1895 showed Goebel the strength of nativist sentiment— sentiment which would not favor an immigrant's son. Weakened by Populist, A.P.A., and gold Democrat defections, the party that had ruled for three decades now lost. Bradley became the state's first Republican governor. Democratic hegemony was shattered. And Goebel had even more problems of his own.

4

"DIVISION AND DISCORD"

WITH HIS SELECTION as leader in the senate in 1894 Goebel seemed to be rising toward his ambition of higher political office. But events over the next two years made such an occurrence seem an utter impossibility. Adversity began innocently enough. In 1894, Goebel sought and expected to receive his party's nomination for a vacant Court of Appeals seat. Factionalism within Goebel's own Democratic party, however, denied him the nomination.

The factionalism, which went back many years, had grown out of severe personal animosities as well as political rivalries. Theodore Hallam and Harvey Myers, Jr. were longtime foes of Goebel's rising power in Kenton County. An ex-Confederate officer, Hallam, if nothing else, brought forth colorful descriptions. To Irvin Cobb he was "a battered-looking, hard-hitting, hard-drinking little Irish lawyer"; and to an angry, anonymous writer, Hallam had a "moral character [that] would stagger a stone fence—His virtues would be lonesome in a capsule." Hallam's letters reveal a witty, likable man, and his actions show a strong one. Although his high, strident voice did not seem suitable, he was an excellent orator—to Cobb perhaps "the greatest natural orator in a state of natural orators." In addition, he had political power and the ambition—like Goebel—for more. His ties to the L & N and his services as an attorney for the C & O meant that his course and Goebel's pointed toward a collision. Harvey Myers, Jr., the younger member of the firm of Hallam and Myers, had received his legal training under Hallam's guidance. Son of a Republican who had been shot in 1874, Myers had turned to the Democracy and found it receptive. He became speaker of the Kentucky house in 1889–90.

In 1890 powerful divisions, which had long existed in the county, finally surfaced. The occasion came when the Democrats met in convention to select a nominee for Congress, after Carlisle's selection for the Senate. According to later recollections, after over 200 exhausting ballots Hallam lacked only one-fourth vote to receive the nomination. Selection meant virtual election. A reporter went to Goebel and suggested that, as the two men represented the same county, he should give Hallam the needed support. Goebel said no. Exasperated, the reporter said, "Oh, Give it to him." He remembered how Goebel turned, "half-smiling, half-snarling, looking more hate than he could have felt" and sneered, "I'd rather cut his throat." Hallam did not receive the nomination, but he threw his votes to a candidate in opposition to Goebel's choice. Both men had in effect lost that confrontation, but their animosities continued.

In 1891 when Goebel worked for Clay's gubernatorial nomination, Hallam and Myers opposed him. Louisville and Nashville trains carried their supporters to the local convention. Goebel had told his candidate, "I have things well in hand. I do not see how we can be beaten." When the voting began his analysis was verified, and finally Hallam and Myers, defeated and embittered, withdrew from the convention.

It was a third member of the faction, however, who eventually turned the feud from angry words to bloody action. A longtime friend of Hallam's, John L. Sanford (also spelled Sandford) was an ex-Confederate who had served under the Kentucky idols of the Confederacy—generals John Hunt Morgan, William Preston, Humphrey Marshall, and John C. Breckinridge. Related both to the Breckinridge clan and to the Marshalls, Sanford turned from a formal political career to become cashier and chief officer of Covington's Farmers' and Traders' National Bank. He still kept his interest and influence in the political sphere, however. Goebel and Sanford clashed on various issues, including ones involving Kenton County toll roads. It was Sanford who received credit for blocking Goebel's attempt to secure the appellate judgeship. An angry William Goebel secretly purchased a Covington newspaper, the *Ledger*, to voice his opposition to Sanford. An article soon appeared about the attempt by "Gon_h_ea" Sanford to get a pardon for a kinsman in an earlier fraud case.

Later, on 11 April 1895, Goebel and Attorney General W. J. "Jack" Hendricks were walking toward Sanford's bank to cash Hendricks's check. They met Frank P. Helm, president of the rival First National Bank, and on Goebel's suggestion they started for Helm's bank. As they approached the building, Helm saw Sanford on the steps and noted that fact to Goebel. "Yes," the senator said, "there the ———— ." Hendricks was introduced to Sanford, whom he had never met. The banker shook hands with his left hand and kept the right one in his pocket. Goebel had his right hand in his pants pocket as well. Both men remained aloof and cool.

Turning to Goebel, Sanford said, "I understand that you assume the authorship of that article."

"I do," acknowledged Goebel.

Quickly two shots rang out. Helm, so close that he suffered powder burns, looked at both men, who for an instant remained perfectly still. Then he saw blood trickle from Sanford's forehead, and the banker fell forward. Shot through the head, Sanford lived only a few hours. Goebel looked at the mortally wounded man, placed the pistol back in his pocket, and calmly walked off. He went directly to police headquarters, phoned his brother Justus, turned to the law officials, and declared, "Well, I suppose you have heard of it." Surrendering, he turned over a .38 Smith & Wesson revolver with one empty chamber. Then Goebel went into the chief of police's private office, where he was soon joined by the mayor and by Justus. For two and a half hours the group remained secluded. After posting the required bond, Goebel went home. At the preliminary hearing Goebel casually opened his mail and did not indicate any uncertainty over his guilt or innocence. After hearing the testimony, the judge dismissed the charges, since "reasonable doubt" existed.

Only two witnesses saw the shooting. Neither Hendricks nor Helm could say who drew first. Hendricks suggested that Sanford did; Helm surmised that this was "possibly" the case, since Sanford had fallen first. Both did agree that the two shots were fired almost simultaneously, as quickly as two snaps of a finger. Based on the testimony, there is no real evidence on who fired the first shot. Both men obviously expected trouble. As Sanford's friends noted later, he was an excellent shot; yet at close range his bullet missed Goebel completely, passing through his coat and trousers. Sanford could have drawn first, yet have made a fatal error, and Goebel could have reacted quickly. There simply is no way of knowing who should be held responsible.

It is certain, however, that Goebel received highly favorable treatment from the courts, both then and later. After the initial reversal by a factional ally of Goebel's, Hallam and company would not let the matter go without one last attempt to ruin Goebel. Three years later, in 1898, Hallam represented the widow in an attempt to sue Goebel for $100,000. Judge James P. Tarvin's rulings openly favored the defense and Goebel escaped unscathed. But the whole affair left Goebel's political world in chaos. Powerful United States Senator J. C. S. Blackburn, whom Goebel had not supported and who was a close friend of the dead man, vowed eternal and earthly revenge. In his eulogy of Sanford he concluded, "I shall make it my life's mission to avenge him by burying his slayer in the depths of merited public execration." As the copper-lined casket was lowered into the ground, with it went many of Goebel's hopes for statewide support.

To his opposition, Goebel had become a murderer. The man who had once said that "the age of dueling is as dead as the age of chivalry" had, in effect, fought a duel; but one without either honor or chivalry—which made it even more unpalatable to aristocratic Kentuckians. The article that had triggered the entire incident was a scurrilous political attack that offended even Goebel's friends. To add to the Kenton County senator's woes, Sanford had been a devoted ex-Confederate. His murder by the son of a Union veteran would not soon be forgotten, or forgiven, by his fellow ex-Confederates. Sanford's widow, General Marshall's niece, had to be placed in an insane asylum; and newspapers noted that she had gradually lost her reason "ever since the awful shock occasioned by the bringing home of her husband's bloody dead body." Confederate censure solidified in opposition to Goebel.

Reporters suddenly noticed that after the last legislative session, Goebel had lost his following: "Recognizing this and smarting under it, he was becoming all the fiercer in his opposition to measures he did not approve and more curt toward persons whom he suspected of being unfriendly to his views." Once dictator of the senate, Goebel could no longer control that body, they declared. Whether theirs was a correct assessment or not, Goebel had certainly lost much support. In the next few months his candidate for governor failed to receive the nomination. Goebel's ambitions and reforms now seemed unattainable.

For a long time, even before first running for senator, Goebel had been building a strong organization. By the early 1890s he could challenge and overcome Hallam and Myers through the machine he had assembled. Acknowledging his personal shortcomings as a stump politician, Goebel had been forced to rely on organization to ensure election. His proficiency in the political arena stamped him as a first-class professional, with little time for idealism. He combined the "gut-fighting tactics of a political boss" with the issue-oriented politics of the people's advocate. Goebel built a machine and functioned as a classic political boss. But he always recognized that to win he needed the vote of the masses, which required such an issue as the regulation of railroads. Goebel began to collect old political debts, he strengthened his machine, and he effected an intricate series of political maneuvers that showed his consummate political skill. "Boss Bill" began to make his way back from predicted political oblivion.

After a caucus vote of 15-6 Goebel again won the Democratic nomination for president pro tem of the senate and he easily defeated his Republican opponent. He thus survived his first test following the 1895 defeats. The question of extreme interest in January 1896, however, was the election of a United States senator. The gold issue dominated discussion. Giants in the Democratic party stood firmly opposed to the popular free silver movement and their opposition threatened to make them party outcasts. New Departure Democrats Watterson and Breckinridge bitterly attacked all inflationary schemes, while Carlisle became, to Ben Tillman of South Carolina, the "Judas from Kentucky" because of his Treasury Department efforts for the gold standard. Clay, Senator William Lindsay, former Governor Buckner, and other prominent leaders refused to yield to agrarian demands. Election of a senator would be a test of strength for the two sides. Goebel gave no real indication that he favored either side. He probably saw the whole issue—with some correctness—as a diversion that could only hurt any chances his reform measures might have. Yet he recognized that the issue could destroy political influence, or even a career.

As the Democratic legislative caucus prepared to meet to choose their nominee for senator, newspapers speculated on the Kenton County senator's course. James B. McCreary, former governor and an ex-Confederate colonel under Morgan, was one hopeful; Goebel attended one of his conferences, leaving the impression of support. But "Bothsides" McCreary had a deserved reputation of not taking stands on issues and of following rather than leading. Such indecisiveness did not appeal to Goebel. Still, he left McCreary feeling that he had Goebel's support.

Former Governor Brown and Goebel had somehow mended their relations. Newspapers now reported that Goebel supported Brown for the senate. In the first caucus vote that was Goebel's position. Again he had backed a loser, for Brown received only 6 votes and McCreary but 13. The third contender received 37 votes and the nomination. "Jo" Blackburn, the man who had pledged to avenge Sanford's death not a year earlier, was the party's choice. Or at least he was the free silver choice, for gold Democrats refused to participate in the caucus, and their votes would be necessary for election.

Goebel's dilemma was obvious. If he did not go for Blackburn in a race expected to be very close, his vote might cost the Democrats a senate seat. Blackburn, ever ambitious, saw as much. The two men met, discussed earlier problems and current issues, and pledged support for each other. Such a move was political strategy at its best, for each man desperately needed the other. Goebel's sole vote, plus his senate influence, could bring Blackburn back to the United States Senate. And as "Old Jo" now led the majority agrarians in the state Democratic party, his support would heal party divisions and prove of future usefulness. The two men ignored the past as if it had never happened. Blackburn ended by praising— not burying—Goebel.

On the first ballot for senator, on 22 January 1896, Blackburn received 58 votes, including Goebel's, but he did not win. No one did. Republican candidate Dr. W. Godfrey "Gumshoe" Hunter received all but one of his party's votes. Though the Republicans controlled the house, on joint ballot the two parties were almost evenly divided. Nine gold Democrats, however, refused to support the free silver views of Blackburn; they cast their ballots for McCreary, Carlisle, and Buckner. When the final results were announced, Hunter lacked one vote to win nomination.

And so began a long and bitter selection process that would continue for 112 ballots and would not be decided for fifteen more months. Hunter remained only one or two votes from victory, but he could never get a majority; while the gold Democrats continued to support their principles over their party, scattering votes among different "sound money" men. Blackburn could not win without their votes, which they would not surrender. Through it all Goebel went with "Old

Jo." Every vote was sought, almost every appeal was made. Talk of bribery spread and partisanship grew even stronger. Silverites challenged Dr. Hunter's citizenship, for he had been born in England; but that issue got nowhere. Then came a partisan grand jury indictment of Hunter for bribery. He was quickly acquitted. Several elections had been contested, and in March the reports were issued. In the Republican-controlled house one Democrat lost his seat; in the Democratic senate two Republicans lost on weak grounds. When the two ousted Republicans sought to vote in the senatorial contest, armed Blackburn partisans guarded the doors to refuse them entry. Bloodshed almost resulted. Outside, supporters of both sides roamed the streets, angry and ready to give support to their parties. To Henry Watterson's avowedly prejudiced eyes, "turbulence, ruffianism, madness, anarchy, reigned." Such actions by civilized leaders of a state were an outrage, "a mockery of civilization, a prostitution of political methods to the ends of insane partisanship and brutish barbarism."

In this explosive atmosphere Governor Bradley ordered out nearly 400 militia, to guard and to occupy the Capitol. Although calm was quickly restored, Democrats attacked the decision. Republican actions in the South during Reconstruction had given the party a reputation in the state for quick use of military force. To Democrats Bradley's order confirmed that reputation, and so on 16 March 1896 a senate committee investigated the governor's call for militia. Goebel chaired the committee and took a leading role in the questioning. While the investigation continued, Goebel introduced a resolution which set guilt on the Republicans for not consulting civil authorities and for acting only "to bring about the election of the Republican candidate for United States senator." It declared that the use of force was "unnecessary" and "solely for partisan political purposes." The resolution passed 19-14.

The committee then heard Bradley testify. The governor scoffed at the whole affair, noting that "guilt" had been established before the evidence was heard. He said that the committee's work smacked of a star-chamber investigation for which there was no defense. He noted that his order to the adjutant general read, "The General Assembly . . . must be allowed to control the legislation without interference, dictation, or intimidation from any source." State officials continued to be admitted to the chambers, he pointed out. After a heated question and answer session, Goebel shouted to Bradley: "We will not be intimidated by either the Governor or the militia."

"Neither is the Governor being intimidated by you," Bradley firmly declared.

The quieter times that followed did not change the voting, and regular adjournment came without a decision on the senate seat. Since the Democrats had refused to appropriate sufficient funds, and since no election for senator had resulted, Bradley called a special session in March 1897. Virtually the same count resulted, with Hunter still lacking those few votes and the "sound money" Democrats backing anyone except Blackburn. A compromise candidate could have given the victory to the Democracy, but neither Blackburn nor Goebel would yield. The balloting continued for two more months.

Hunter finally stepped aside, and Republicans selected a relatively unknown state legislator. On 28 April 1897, W. J. Deboe became Kentucky's first Republican senator. Goebel had gambled in supporting Blackburn. But he had done so with the expectation that "Old Jo" would win and that, in victory, he would aid Goebel's ambitions. Though Goebel now would not have the patronage that a senator could give him, he still had gained a valuable and popular ally for the future.

After the disasters of 1895 Goebel had made peace with his powerful opponents Brown and Blackburn, and he had gained additional statewide support by these associations. But in his home county of Kenton the power struggle continued, and Goebel needed a victory over Hallam and Myers there to indicate his strength to any doubters. Winning would require a careful and calculated maneuver that few Kentucky politicians besides Goebel could execute. His friendship with "sound money" men such as Clay and Carlisle had stamped Goebel as a gold man. His dalliance with McCreary had reinforced that belief, for the former governor was reputed to support "sound money," though, as usual, he was careful not to commit himself. Then had come Goebel's strange alliance with the free silver hero "Jo" Blackburn. He had seemingly gone to the silverites. Not so, Goebel told Carlisle as he asked for support. Walter B. Haldeman, manager of the *Courier-Journal* and the *Louisville Times*, had urged the two men to meet and discuss their views. Carlisle later revealed that Goebel pledged his devotion to "sound money," and said that his support for Blackburn came from personal and party motives, not from philosophical ones.

Writing to an important politician, Goebel explained that if he was to be reelected in 1897 control of the state delegation "is essential." Nothing should obscure the fact, he emphasized, that it was solely a question of "whether I or Myers should control the party machinery of this county." What Goebel wanted—and got—was for Carlisle to support Goebel's delegation to the state convention against Myers's contesting delegation. Assured that his former law partner would oppose free silver, Carlisle used his influence for him, and Goebel won. In doing so he secured his strength among northern Kentuckians. At the convention Goebel then voted for the free silver chairman.

That fall Goebel's course could be clearly discerned by all involved. William Jennings Bryan's nomination by the national Democratic party at Chicago threw the "sound money" forces into total opposition. Tainted by the "anarchist" Populists, embracing free silver completely, Bryan could not be supported by the upper echelons of a fading Bourbon-New Departure leadership. The list of Bryan's opponents in Kentucky read like the master roll of powerful politicians— Buckner, Watterson, Breckinridge, Lindsay, Carlisle, Clay. Active in support of a third party, the so-called gold Democrats, this group proclaimed theirs the "true" party, and Bryan's but a bastard undeserving of recognition. A free silver advocate suggested in return that the gold Democrats, like the mule, were "without pride of ancestry or hope of posterity."

"Sound money" advocates had leaders, but few followers. Watterson's *Courier-Journal* proclaimed "No compromise with dishonor," but found its circulation falling dangerously low. The free silver panacea attracted mass support—and votes. With agrarians in control, it was now the old leadership who turned to third parties. Goebel supported Bryan's campaign and, in doing so, at last completely repudiated his ties to the old order and to Carlisle. As the old leaders passed, Goebel had enough influence and power to move ahead on his own, and he made the necessary alliances—chiefly with Blackburn—to gain further strength.

Election results did not yield the expected and usual Democratic victory. Bryan lost the state to McKinley by 281 votes. The gold Democratic vote, though small (5,108 votes), may have decided the contest for the Republicans. Conservative Democrats in old Whig centers, especially in the Bluegrass, refused to support the party. In the poorer, mountain sections of the state Bryan's small-farmer appeal found little sympathy, as these normally Republican areas increased their usual majorities. Four counties, in fact, cast more than 100 percent of their eligible votes. In the rural areas of western Kentucky, stronghold of Democratic and Populist strength, Bryan found his greatest support. But it was not enough.

More upsetting for Goebel was growing Republican strength in urban areas—a national trend—since here lay Goebel's political base and chief hope for gaining strength. The party of McKinley reversed Louisville's usual Democratic majority to a 60 percent Republican vote. Republicans carried the city for the first time in thirty years. They also reduced the Democratic majority in Kenton County to a very narrow margin. The Republican threat became even more evident in Goebel's own reelection campaign the next year. Goebel won in 1897, but the three-to-one margin of four years before had disappeared. The final tally of 5,795 to 5,095 votes was surprisingly close.

Yet the fact that he won reelection itself indicates that Goebel had recovered from his temporary setbacks. All that had occurred over the past two years—Sanford's death and the resulting ex-Confederate disenchantment, Goebel's defeat for the Court of Appeals seat, Republican victories in 1895 and 1896, Blackburn's defeat for the senate, Goebel's reputation as a machine politician, Carlisle's break with his former partner—made it seem almost impossible that William Goebel could advance politically. But Goebel would not abandon his search for power. The old leaders had been seriously crippled by the free silver issue and by their support for railroads. Into that leadership void Goebel entered, as he sought to become the spokesman for the still-leaderless masses.

Goebel wanted the governorship that would be decided in 1899. The process that culminated in nomination usually began at least a year before the convention, as hopefuls wrote letters asking for each county's support. Goebel started much earlier, since to create any opportunity for the nomination he had not only to control the legislature for enactment of his reform measures, but also to attract significant mass attention and support.

Throughout the difficult years of 1895 to 1897, Goebel had continued to push for needed reforms. One of his proposals sought to make women eligible for the office of school trustee, for membership on the Board of Education, and for voting for these offices. On 2 April 1897, Goebel's bill passed the senate, but it failed later in the house. As in earlier sessions, Goebel also spoke and acted against lotteries and poolrooms. On such issues he appealed more to middle- and upper-class reformers than to Populists and rural farmers, who had little sympathy for the women's rights movement. But Goebel's growing image as a machine politician alienated Progressives and thus negated some possible support.

During this same period Goebel grew more concerned about the "evils" of Republicanism. Bradley's conduct in the senatorial race stamped him, to Goebel's view, as the leader of a party that would do anything to win. Republican victory in the 1896 presidential race, Goebel suggested, had resulted from fraud, and—whether he was correct or not—this belief strengthened his determination to oppose their every move. The L & N's growing inclination to support the now majority party convinced him of the Republican evils. And the findings of a partisan legislative committee investigating state prisons in 1897 cemented that outlook.

The penitentiary system in Kentucky had long been a disgrace. In the late 1870s nearly 1,000 prisoners had been crowded into cells designed to hold 780. Each of these cells measured less than four feet wide and seven feet long. The annual mortality rate sometimes approached 10 percent. A governor who had sought to reform the system cried out that the "Black Hole of Calcutta . . . was not much worse than this." Since then the system had been marked with fraud, callousness, and little substantive reform. Investigations under Democratic governors had taken place much earlier, but Goebel had had no part in those. Now sitting in judgment on the Republicans, Goebel blamed them for everything; and—as in past Democratic administrations—he found justified grounds for complaint. Testimony, often of conflicting nature, told of women prisoners going to men's barracks at night, punishment with thumbscrews, whippings with a two-inch strap, sodomy, food filled with maggots. The affair confirmed his belief that corporational power had touched the Republicans and corrupted them.

The reform measures, the investigation, and related events still had not brought Goebel's name before the people to any degree. Although he functioned as senate party leader, out in the state others filled the leadership vacuum created by the defection of gold Democrats and the absence of a Democratic governor. If Goebel hoped to achieve enough recognition to overcome his handicaps in time for the gubernatorial canvass, he would have to realize that hope in the 1898 legislative session. The Democracy had swept to victory in the fall elections and controlled both houses. Bradley's programs had no chance of enactment; "Boss Bill" Goebel's programs would. In the senate the lieutenant governor was virtually stripped of his appointive powers by a party vote. Reelected senate president pro tem by a 26-8 vote, Goebel, "The Kenton King," ruled supreme.

Goebel was more active in the senate than ever before, and

his strongest efforts were devoted to party measures. Although he did push for restriction of convict labor, tighter regulation of doctors, and "free" toll roads, Goebel focused his attention on other measures, one of which was the so-called fellow-servant bill. Long interested in such a measure, the senator sought to change existing laws that made individual employees—not the railroad company—liable if an injury was suffered by one worker through another's negligence. As Goebel envisioned it, the owners ("masters") should be financially responsible for the negligence of their "servants and fellow servants." A similar measure assigned joint responsibility for all actions against and liabilities of "master and servant, employer and employee." Both measures passed, but Bradley vetoed the fellow-servant bill after the session had ended.

A second pet project did not even get to the governor. Goebel's close friend J. Morton Chinn introduced a bill that sought to end a textbook company's monopoly by setting a uniform price, with penalties for variances. Conservatives saw in the measure an attempt to restrict free enterprise and perhaps even to set up another monopoly as well. Many Democrats shared the Republicans' reservations about the wisdom of state interference in such matters. The Chinn bill failed, and a milder substitute could not get out of a joint committee.

If conservative elements feared the "interference" of the Chinn bill, then the McChord bill terrified them. Drafted by a former railroad commissioner and member of the constitutional convention, the proposal gave the railroad commission power to hear evidence and to "determine a just and reasonable rate." If the commission found the railroads guilty of "unjust discrimination" they could be fined. Influential Democratic newspapers either joined the Republican press's opposition or ignored the issue editorially. Goebel spoke and worked behind the scene to insure passage of the measure. He noted how other states had similar laws and he stressed the need for tighter railroad control. Finally in a Democratic caucus he got the bill endorsed as a party measure. Although not all Democrats fell in line, enough did so to pass the McChord bill.

On 28 February 1898, Bradley vetoed the bill, citing the "arbitrary, absolute and final" decision it granted to the commissioners. With such "unbridled power" in their hands, they were taking property without any redress. Yes, corporate power should be held in check, Bradley admitted, but not in this manner. Allow review and further appeal, he urged. Repeating Bradley's arguments, many "New South" Democratic editors agreed that the powers granted were too vast, that the object of government was protection of property, not seizure of it. Goebel Democrats reminded them of the influence wielded by the L & N in the friendly courts and of the need for tighter control of what they saw as a dangerous monopoly. But apparently the opposition found receptive listeners, for the senate failed to override the veto, as ten Democrats deserted their party. On all three measures the Goebel Democrats had failed to enact their goals, and their efforts had alienated many others in their party. The fourth measure would increase tensions almost to the breaking point.

On 1 February 1898 Goebel himself had introduced "an act to further regulate elections." Since his days at the constitutional convention the senator had been interested in changing election laws. The system in use when he acted gave county officials the power to select their area's election officers. In this way local party realities were recognized. Where Democrats made up the county court they dominated; where Republicans did, they had control. Final decisions were left to a state canvassing board composed of high elected officials.

The Goebel election bill sought radical change in the entire system. A central state election board would be set up with three members, selected by legislative vote, as the final judge of all contests. More important, perhaps, these commissioners would select the county election boards, who in turn would choose the precinct officials. No provision was made for equal party representation except at the precinct level. The legislature, then Democratic, replaced the executive, then Republican, as the source of ultimate decision. Goebel defended the bill, saying that Republican fraud in the 1896 presidential election justified such a move. He stressed that this was a reform measure.

One explanation for Goebel's bill is that his motives were entirely noble. Seeing fraud, and innocently oblivious to any similar occurrences in his own party, Goebel sought simply to clean up state elections, according to this view; and the bill fit well with his reform orientation. Such a view is, at best, charitable. It probably is incorrect. Both sides had used methods in previous elections that had violated the code of honest political conduct. Irregularities in 1896 were probably little or no worse than in earlier years. Democrats had been as guilty as Republicans; no conspiracy existed. As one Democrat wrote a few years later, "It [the Goebel bill] assumed that the standard of integrity in the Democratic party was a very high one, and that the interests of good and honest government could safely be intrusted to its custody and control. It also assumed, on the other hand, that the standard of integrity in the Republican party was doubtful. . . . These were very arbitrary assumptions." Goebel's real motivation may have been the fact that the Republicans had successfully challenged his party's dominance. For whatever the rhetoric, the bill's chief aim was to keep the Democracy supreme. Many reformers found the bill distasteful and saw little evidence of its reform spirit. On the contrary, to many in both parties the law was the antithesis of reform. To them it would set up dictatorial boss rule and one-man politics. Reaction to the bill came quickly.

New Departure leader W. C. P. Breckinridge and his son Desha, who would be one of the leaders of the Progressive movement in twentieth-century Kentucky, found the bill anathema. As editors of the Lexington *Morning Herald* they equated "Goebelism" with "Bryanism," which they believed had encouraged lawless destruction of toll roads, socialism, and "assault upon the rights of property."

A silver-bearded, stocky, sharp-tongued ex-Confederate, "Willie" Breckenridge could be a formidable opponent. Colonel Breckinridge used his wit and his melodious voice well, and he became one of the most sought-after speakers in the nation. He earned the title "Silver-Tongued Orator from Ken-turcky." Breckinridge had used his talents to gain election to Congress, like his grandfather and cousins before him. He had served for a decade, until a scandal cut short his career. He then turned to journalism and proclaimed the "New South" vision for Kentucky through the columns of his paper. A party outcast for his "sound money" views, he used his consider-able talents to oppose this upstart, Goebel, whose background so varied with his own. He and Goebel represented two dif-ferent political worlds.

The *Herald* had cautioned its readers earlier to beware of these new leaders, men "who would fain be considered gen-tlemen." Now it warned of the dangers involved in this "Force Bill" which centralized power and ended home rule. Demo-crats would not accept it, even if it was forced through the legislature by the "Kenton Czar." If reforms were needed, this bill provided no solution, but rather "a simple, efficient and powerful machine to declare the desired persons elected." Breckinridge predicted—accurately—that soon "we may have two distinct Legislatures, two rival Governors . . . each claim-ing recognition of the Federal Administration." This problem could be avoided by strong leaders, but he saw before him only "poor weaklings in the Legislature whose backbone is mush and whose liver is white; who know what is right, but are too cowardly to stand up for their convictions and cower be-hind the hypocritical pretenses of caucus and regularity, poor, poor fellows!"

In Louisville "Marse Henry" Watterson viewed matters similarly. Vain, talented, cantankerous, blind in one eye, prid-ing himself on his cultural tastes, the editor of the *Courier-Journal* yielded nothing to Breckinridge when it came to in-tense opposition to Goebel. Although his paper's sagging circulation had dictated that he in fact compromise with "dis-honor" and support the free silver Democrats, Watterson still had no use for their new leader. He branded Goebel's bill "of imminent and deadly peril to the state." The ex-Confederate son of a Tennessee congressman asked legislators to repudiate this measure "of sweeping viciousness and far-reaching evil."

The author of the measure wants to be governor, said Watterson, and sees in this "a ready chariot to bear him thither." Men should not follow this "slayer of civil liberty." But Watterson's faith in the party indicated to him that the election law would not pass: "The Democrats of Kentucky have not sunk so low as that."

Other party leaders spoke out against the proposal, including P. P. Johnston, the chairman of the state central committee. In the senate a former ally and friend of Goebel's turned to bitter opposition. Charles J. Bronston had served in the constitutional convention and on various senate committees with the Kenton legislator. Like Goebel, a onetime law partner of a governor—in this case McCreary—Bronston was able, bold, resourceful, and aggressive. Disliking the centralizing tendencies of the bill, he attacked it on the floor as a measure "not only subversive of our republican system of local government, but [also] . . . a confession of cowardice."

Despite opposition, the Goebel election bill passed the senate 20-15, with four Democrats, including Bronston, and two Populists joining the minority Republicans. After a caucus endorsement, on 26 February 1898 the bill passed the house by a 57-42 vote, with more than a dozen Democrats in opposition.

The Republican Lexington *Daily Leader* saw this action as "the enthronement of Goebel as boss and absolute dictator of Kentucky politics." Only a "virtuous veto" by Bradley could "save the honor" of Kentuckians. Watterson's *Courier-Journal* proclaimed "All Hail, King Goebel!" Watterson also stressed the strength Goebel and his supporters had: "With party law of their own making drawn taut and trim, with warrants of political death to all who refuse submission . . . a Triumvirate, controlled by a Dictator, is ordained and established."

Republican Bradley echoed Democrat Watterson in a long veto message filled with legal opinions. "Billy O. B." declared the bill unconstitutional and he saw power centralized in "a triumvirate that has more power than any court." His veto was overridden, and the Goebel election bill became law. Unfriendly legislators hailed "William the Conqueror."

But in this bill Goebel had made his gravest political error. Although it certainly attracted the attention he needed from both the press and the people, the bill had won him few new allies and would cost him many supporters. Conservatives feared its centralization of powers, while reformers considered it dictatorial boss politics of the foulest sort. Goebel could have pursued the gubernatorial nomination without the bill. But he wanted final victory too much. His tendency to over-estimate the evil in those who opposed him caused Goebel to expect the worst from them. To his thinking, the bill was needed to insure his expected election—and that was motive enough.

Ironically, after Goebel's death, Bronston suggested that the Goebel bill in fact had not originated with its sponsor. According to Bronston, Goebel acknowledged his desire to become governor, so that he could control corporate excesses and unify and standardize internal affairs. To gain allies Goebel had made many commitments, one of which was to support an election bill. Bronston argued that the Kenton County senator had reluctantly introduced the proposal for an ally. Coming when it did, close to Goebel's death, Bronston's story is suspect. Goebel spoke of "my bill" in debates, and he argued very forcibly for it. He did nothing to discourage identification of himself with the bill. And he expected to use it to his benefit. Still, the basic theme does not change: Goebel sought the office of governor and would use the Goebel bill as a vehicle to accomplish that goal.

After passage of the bill, the legislature met to appoint the three electoral commissioners. The Republicans walked out, refusing to take part in the selection of men for such an odious board. Goebel surprised his critics, and strengthened his claim that this was a reform measure, by choosing three able men. The legislature unanimously confirmed the appointments of William S. Pryor, Charles B. Poyntz, and William T. Ellis. Pryor, the most distinguished of the three, had served on the Court of Appeals for two and a half decades before his recent election defeat by a Republican. The seventy-three year old Confederate sympathizer was well respected. Poyntz, a much younger man, had entered politics only recently, after operating a wholesale whiskey business. A term in the state senate had been followed by appointment to the Railroad Commission, where he sat until the Republicans came in. Ellis, on the other hand, had entered politics shortly after his return from the Civil War. Following a Harvard education, his career included stints in Congress. Although men of high character, the appointees were nevertheless devoted Goebel supporters who had experienced recent defeats by Republicans. They appointed two Democrats and one Republican to each county commission. Local party strength would be replaced by Democratic control.

Angry Republicans had already determined that in Goebel they had a bitter enemy; the board's action confirmed that analysis. Democrats who had split over the virtues of the election bill before its passage still debated its wisdom. As the head of the Democratic State Central Committee wrote, "What a strong commanding position we held until this legislature met. Now division and discord."

5

"THERE IS GOING TO BE A HOT FIGHT"

IN NOVEMBER 1898, William Goebel wrote to his brother Justus about the political situation as he began formal campaigning for governor. Living an almost puritanical life himself, the older brother moralistically attacked two Covington politicians as drunkards who spent all their time in pool halls and at racetracks. The next mayor must be an enemy of these men, he wrote, for "I shall not permit any man to be elected Mayor on the Democratic ticket unless he is entirely satisfactory to me. I shall beat any man that I do not like with the Election Commission. I turned over to [J. W.?] Pugh the entire matter of appointing election officers this year. Next year I shall attend to the matter myself, whether I am nominated for governor, or not.

"There is going to be a hot fight between me and Hardin for the nomination."

And there was. Goebel's chief rival, "Wat" Hardin, had been running for governor for almost a decade. He had lost the nomination in 1891; won it in 1895, and then lost the election. Now he was making his final effort. The tall, handsome, former state attorney general had served the Bourbon-New Departure Democrats well, until his turn to free silver left some feeling betrayed. He still controlled the regular party organizations, however, and of all three serious candidates he came closest to what the L & N wanted. Hardin thus gained their important support and many benefits.

Hardin's opposition to Goebel was stated best by the paper his allies purchased to proclaim his cause. The *Louisville Dispatch* asked why not Goebel, and answered, "because he is not a man of the people; because he has none of the chivalrous spirit of a Kentuckian; because he is selfish and a demagogue; . . . because he holds that it is legitimate politics to plunder the public; because he will sacrifice friend or party to self-interest; because he has no ability beyond trickery." They pictured William Goebel as an undemocratic, unchivalrous, ambitious, dangerous demagogue. More quietly they attacked his origins and background.

While Hardin's strength lay in the party organization, in central Kentucky, and among businessmen, a third contender spoke for the powerful agrarians, chiefly centered in western Kentucky. William J. Stone had most of the prerequisites for victory. He had lost a leg in the war while serving the Confederacy; on his return he had entered politics, had risen to become speaker of the Kentucky house, and was elected to Congress. The bewhiskered farmer and former Granger had tremendous appeal in the west, and his opposition to the L & N was well known. Captain Stone's candidacy took from Goebel much of his expected antirailroad support.

And Goebel was worried. Writing again to Justus in late February 1899, the despondent candidate found enemies all around. Persons "pretending to be friends" had destroyed all his chances to be governor. He spoke of withdrawing, for "I know I can not be nominated." The "blood-suckers" had done their work well. A few days later he wrote of his expectation that he would soon retire from the race as he cared nothing for the governorship. "I am better off without it." A postscript to this letter suggested, however, that his protests might not be what they appeared. He added, "The Louisville crowd is no good to me, and I want to smash them anyhow." These letters came at a low point in Goebel's canvass and represented more a rationalization than a correct indication of his mood. For Goebel's strong will would not allow him to surrender so easily. He fought back.

Goebel still had powerful allies. He had toured the state in August of the previous year and gathered support. Blackburn had conferred with him and apparently agreed on at least a temporary alliance. Walter B. Haldeman, publisher of the *Courier-Journal* and the *Louisville Times*, although publicly neutral, supported Goebel; while his perplexed editor, Henry Watterson, pondered what possible course he could take. Although Stone's candidacy had destroyed Goebel's expectation of carrying the western part of the state, the man from Kenton felt reasonably certain that he could still do well elsewhere, especially in northern Kentucky. And although Hardin had much of the organizational support, Goebel sat on both the state central and state executive committees and he had friends there as well.

Goebel's strength was urban. Stone's lay in rural areas, while Hardin's was more diverse. The northern Kentucky candidate had to get some significant support from rural areas, which predominated in Kentucky. A Hardin newspaper, the *Woodford Sun*, taunted Goebel on this very fact: "Mr. Goebel's machine politics do very well in the city, but they can't be worked on country folks." In an effort to overcome this drawback Goebel spoke in rural areas to appeal for support. At Bedford on 30 May 1899, he replied to Hardin's attacks. "I have not had a powerful family connection nor wealth to aid me," he told a predominately small-farmer crowd. "I am not the chance bearer of a great name made famous by somebody else." Instead, he stressed, he was of humble origin. He attacked the "Frankfort dynasty," to which Hardin belonged, as a producer of "Tateism."

Goebel had also declared his support for the Chinn and McChord bills and for the election law, but the talk was clearly defensive. In that he succeeded well, and several of his speeches were distributed in quantities of 40–50,000 throughout the state. Friendly newspapers like the *Glasgow Times* called for bold measures, as advocated by Goebel. "The

Democratic party in Kentucky is in the supremest peril in its existence," asserted the editor. "The battle of its life is just before it." The candidacy of Goebel represented the forces of good against corporational influence and must be supported.

There was, of course, danger in this approach. Portraying opponents as evil significantly lessened chances that the three hopefuls could unite later in a harmonious battle against the Republicans. Breckinridge cautioned against this very danger in April, warning that "the personal assaults are . . . sowing noxious seeds from which divisions, heart-burnings and feuds will spring." Hardin, Goebel, and Stone would reap the results.

In Louisville the bitterness of a local primary had made suspect that city's devotion to the Democracy. Two local factions, as in Covington, had long fought for power. One side, including Watterson, Haldeman, and the incumbent mayor, opposed a group headed by Louisville's own boss, ex-Confederate John Whallen. Owner of the famous Buckingham burlesque theater, Whallen used "the Buck" as a center of operations. From there he supervised various legal and illegal enterprises, aided the needy—in exchange for their vote—and in 1899 joined forces with the L & N and the *Louisville Dispatch* to oppose his young rival, William Goebel.

On the day of the primary, before noon, the Whallen-backed Democratic committee declared the election "null and void." They cited "fraudulent interference" by the police and other supporters of the mayor—who aided Goebel. Haldeman's *Courier-Journal* blamed the disruptions on Whallen's forces, who, it argued, saw that they were losing and pulled out. Other men took their places at the polls and voting continued. Soon after, the *Louisville Dispatch* declared that such actions by "Goebel's gamblers" and the mayor's henchmen would not work in future elections. Calling the mayor "a venal character . . . , a cowardly inciter of riot, a disturber of the peace, a highwayman . . . , a man sunk to the lowest depths of political if not moral depravity," the paper suggested that citizens "armed with Winchesters and well supplied with ammunition" be at the polls next time—in the governor's race—

in order to preserve order. If this "gang of political cutthroats" sought to seize power through force they would be disappointed. Goebel, or whoever won the nomination, could not afford to see Louisville go strongly Republican again, but acrimony among its leaders made that an increasing possibility. And such appeals to force meant that both sides, in the long run, would be the losers.

Results of all the various county mass conventions left Goebel trailing both opponents. Hardin needed less than 200 of the large number of uncommitted delegates to secure the 547 necessary for a majority. While the Lexington *Morning Herald* proudly proclaimed that it was "impossible" now for the "Kenton King" to win, other editors were less certain. "That trickery will be resorted to in the coming convention," suggested the *Hazel Green Herald*, ". . . is as plain as the handwriting on the wall."

What initially occurred was less "trickery" than simple, legitimate political strategy and power politics. Both Stone and Goebel opposed the L & N; each expected to receive the votes of western Kentucky should he be nominated; both knew that, if left alone, Hardin would eventually win the contest. Newspapers reported the possibility of an agreement before the delegates even assembled. Then on 21 June 1899, headlines proclaimed: "Stone-Goebel Deal Made."

What had occurred seriously crippled Hardin's chances. One of Stone's managers, the tall, talented, youthful, heavyset orator Ollie James, had called on Goebel's friends and arranged a conference. James and the ambitious leader of Logan County Democrats, John S. Rhea, met with Goebel's representatives, including Owensboro newspaper editor and former railroad commissioner Urey Woodson. After preliminary discussions they broke up and Woodson asked his candidate to meet Stone personally. Goebel left the Galt House in Louisville after midnight and returned three hours later. The excited candidate told a sleepy Woodson (as he later remembered it), "He has agreed to do anything we want, allowing us to name the temporary chairman and promising us his full support." After another meeting a formal agreement was reached. The two men signed a document in Woodson's presence. Goebel pledged to give Stone half of his expected Louisville delegates and to support Stone should Goebel withdraw or be defeated. Stone would reciprocate should he suffer that fate. They agreed to elect the temporary chairman, thus leaving Hardin powerless.

On 21 June, the convention assembled in the Music Hall on Louisville's Market Street. In oppressive heat, the band played "Dixie" over and over again as cheers continued. Finally preliminary business began. P. P. Johnston, a Hardin man, chaired the convention and called for nominations for temporary chairman. The Hardin forces put forth young lawyer William "Roaring Bill" Sweeney. When Stone manager Ollie James rose and presented the name of a Goebelite, David B. Redwine, the convention knew that the rumors of a "deal" were true.

As balloting began, Chairman Johnston ruled on contested delegations, often even hearing evidence. This highly unusual procedure was followed by recognizing delegations certified by established local party officials—the usual procedure. But Johnston at times ruled against these delegations—a very important circumstance for those who had to defend Goebel later. For eight long, hot hours the process went on. The chair had not made an organized effort to throw out Stone or Goebel votes and probably had ruled as it thought just. Johnston had erred, however, by assuming arbitrary powers.

The final results gave the temporary chairmanship, by a very few votes, to the virtually unknown Redwine. The combination had worked. A youthful circuit judge from feud-ridden "Bloody Breathitt," Redwine had served in the legislature concurrently with Goebel and was, wrote the gubernatorial hopeful, "an old friend of mine." Opponents of "Boss Bill" correctly stressed Goebel's complete dominance of Redwine. The chairman did his bidding. In his opening speech Redwine declared that he would see "that every man is accorded a fair hearing," and he added a keynote for the coming campaign: "This is a fight with the people on one side and trusts and corporations on the other." Goebel would not have said it very differently.

Redwine then turned to the most crucial decision of the entire convention: deciding contested delegations. Hardin forces had expected no serious challenges, since they had believed they would elect the chairman and since so many of the contests were from blatantly "rump" conventions. The Committee on Credentials, however, was now composed of a Stone-Goebel majority expected to throw out many opposition votes. The convention adjourned to await their report.

The next day, 23 June, exploded into utter confusion. Headlines screamed: "UNDER CONTROL OF OUTLAWS. Music Hall the Scene of Wild Disorders and Terror, and for a Time on the Verge of Bloodshed." And in this instance reporters were guilty of little exaggeration. Hundreds of nondelegates crowded the floor and arguments broke out. Pistols were drawn and almost used. Who these people were depended on which newspaper you read. To the anti-Hardin *Courier-Journal* most were "Boss" Whallen's "thugs" sent to intimidate, but failing in their mission, because Redwine had gathered plainclothes police to oppose them. The anti-Goebel *Louisville Dispatch* described these men as city police, firemen, and gamblers brought by Goebel to threaten timid, undecided delegates. Whatever their source, the nondelegates confused a badly befuddled situation.

Redwine, as Goebel's ally, postponed any votes until the report of the Committee on Credentials. The convention adjourned that morning, but some 800 people demonstrated their opposition to the tactics that afternoon. Later, when delegates reassembled, Redwine quickly declared the convention adjourned again, since the contested votes had not yet been decided. Charles J. Bronston rose and called for a delegate vote on the adjournment decision. Redwine refused. As some delegates left, Bronston no longer could control his anger at what he saw as the chairman's—and thus Goebel's—utter disregard for parliamentary procedure. To what was described as "a howling mob" of both supporters and opponents, he spoke of this group of "cutthroats and assassins" who thought themselves above the law. He defied the anger of hissing delegates in saying, "I will not be silenced by the outcry of hired thugs who come to this convention armed with brass knuckles and bowie knives. . . . I defy them to silence me." "Roaring Bill" Sweeney told the convention that these men were present "for the purpose of assassination if the opportunity presents." A Republican paper, if anything, underplayed the situation when it said that "utter chaos reigns in the state democratic convention."

And then that night the credentials committee's report was finally submitted. Of the twenty-eight disputed cases, twenty-six were decided in favor of either Goebel or Stone. As a result, Hardin lost almost 160 votes. His forces grew outraged at the decision, shouted for recognition, refused to heed the chair's rulings, and spoke of "czars without conscience," of "traitors without principles."

The next morning the vote came on the Hardin supporters' minority report. Redwine ruled that accredited delegates from contested counties could not vote—thus removing almost one-third of the votes, nearly all for Hardin. The defeat of the minority report by over 100 votes left the Goebel-Stone combination in complete control. Fights broke out on the floor, shouts of anger again filled the hall; but finally Hardin's forces acquiesced, if only grudgingly.

Then, on 24 June, nominations for governor began. Hardin, his face ashen, his hands trembling, walked to the podium, reviewed the contest; and despite shouts of "No! No!" he then withdrew. He recognized the disadvantage the committee report had placed on him. Rhea nominated Stone. Judge Tarvin, who had only recently sat on the Sanford case, put forth Goebel's name.

Stone's managers thought they had an understanding with Goebel that, once Hardin was defeated, he would step down in favor of their candidate. In return, Goebel would be allowed to name other officers and to control party organization. James sent a messenger to Goebel, asking him to withdraw. Goebel refused. "Go tell him, God damn him, to come at once

59

and withdraw," James roared. He then went to tell Goebel himself. The man from northern Kentucky would not step down. James threatened to bolt to Hardin, but Goebel realized how much Stone supporters disliked the L & N's candidate. As his allies warned him of the possible bolt, he answered, "Let them nominate Wat Hardin. If they can stand it, I can." Stone and his delegates could not do that of course; they wanted the governorship too much.

The balloting proceeded quietly enough, until Jefferson County was reached. Louisville's vote, by the prior agreement of the two contenders, was to be divided; but on the roll call all votes went to Goebel. Woodson, who knew of the promised arrangement, pleaded for fulfillment of it. He was laughed at. Every vote was needed by the "Kenton King."

Angry Stone managers, feeling betrayed, began to turn to Hardin, who had received a few loyal votes. It appeared they might select him in order to repay the treachery they thought they saw. Woodson quickly shifted Daviess County's vote, and the votes of five other western Kentucky counties, from Goebel to Stone to try to balance the Louisville turnaround and to appease Stone delegates. Before this move Goebel had lacked less than three dozen votes to win the nomination. Deprived of them, he grew "enraged," according to reporters.

Pandemonium overcame calm discussion, as delegates shouted for attention in the huge hall. County after county changed its vote in the three-hour session. Future governor Augustus Owsley Stanley stood on a box, held on to a chandelier, and announced his county's turn to Hardin. But Woodson had done enough to keep Hardin from gaining a majority. Whereas the first count had been Goebel 520, Stone 428½, and Hardin 126½, the recapitulation gave Stone the lead, Hardin second place, and Goebel third position in a close contest. For eleven more ballots, spread without a break over six hours, this trend continued, with each man holding between 300 and 400 votes. Near midnight the deadlocked convention adjourned for a needed Sunday break.

On Monday delegates reassembled to find the Music Hall filled with over 200 policemen, all there at Redwine's request.

On orders not to allow anybody but delegates and other certified observers on the floor, they refused entrance to some newspaper reporters and, according to anti-Goebel papers, even to some accredited alternates, who had to replace the many tired and disgusted delegates who had returned home.

Rhea asked the chair to remove the police, so that the convention would not be under their control. Redwine declared the motion out of order. An ex-congressman appealed the ruling with the same result. At that, Bronston, Rhea, Sweeney, James, and others exploded. Bronston asked whether any parliamentarian in the hall could support the ruling that no appeal can be made of the chair's decision. All the Hardin and Stone leaders' controlled anger over Redwine's earlier rulings now came into the open.

As Redwine moved to order the balloting to begin, Hardin and Stone delegates hooted and jeered, so that the secretary's voice could not even be heard. Tin horns reinforced voices, and few could hear the chair or the county votes. "The whole floor," one reporter noted, "was a howling, excited pandemonium." Men stood on chairs and shouted at Redwine, and fights started, while Redwine tried to begin the voting. He asked to have those rules read which allowed him to clear the area. James, "his face white with rage," thundered that no rule gave Redwine power to eject delegates. Cries of "Put us out if you can" reinforced him.

"Give us a vote on appeal," the anti-Redwine forces yelled. The chair refused. Another ex-congressman read the rules of order followed in Congress by "Czar" Thomas B. Reed; even the "Czar" allowed an appeal, he pointed out. Redwine ordered the roll called. Songs became popular fare among Hardin and Stone supporters, as they first sang the "Doxology." Sacred music had no soothing influence. Then came "There'll Be a Hot Time in the Old Town Tonight," "My Old Kentucky Home," "Hang Judge Redwine to a Sour Apple Tree" (to the tune of "John Brown's Body") and more. The judge kept time with his gavel.

Voting began, though the results were almost impossible to hear. Many delegations refused to cast their votes. Someone looked at the disorder and sarcastically remarked that Redwine's decision to call in police to keep the peace should bring the convention to thank him "for the good order he is maintaining." For almost an hour the roll was called. Goebel received a majority of those that voted, but two hundred less than an absolute majority.

James asked Redwine if Goebel had received the nomination. The chair answered that he had, and James laughed that such a nomination "would not be worth a baubee [*sic*]!" Goebel realized this too as he observed the proceedings. He passed word to Redwine that a true majority would be required. Meanwhile the convention floor began to resemble a mob scene. For hour after hour the noise and confusion continued, as forces opposed to Goebel and Redwine refused to allow a peaceful vote to take place until the chair gave them a decision on the appeal. Finally, after ten hours and two fruitless ballots, the convention adjourned. To a national press attracted to Goebel since his election law outcry of the year before, this was all good copy. The *New York Times* reported that this "continuous performance of howling farce" called a convention was without doubt "the most uproarious and disorderly body of men ever gathered together for the transaction of political or other business."

The next day the convention seemed composed of a group of men different from those of the day before. Stone and Hardin, still unable to unite their forces, both called later in the day for adjournment to another city. Sweeney asked for a vote on the matter. Redwine, at least consistent, declared the request out of order and refused an appeal. He correctly admitted, "I lay no claim to being a good parliamentarian." This time the forces opposed to Goebel decided to allow the balloting to go on. Each ballot continued close, with less than fifty votes separating the three men. Goebel watched, with Blackburn sometimes at his side, as he trailed Stone and Hardin on both the twentieth and twenty-first ballots. By the twenty-fourth he led by a scant three votes, but the time now was ready for the move that would decide the contest.

A resolution was introduced that called for dropping the

lowest man. Some of the Hardin and Stone leaders were opposed, and one pointed out to Redwine that if this motion
could be voted on, then so too should the earlier call for adjournment. Redwine allowed the vote on the resolution. Tired
delegates, anxious to return to the homes they had left a week
before, narrowly adopted the motion.

The next ballot decided who would be the final contestants
and, surprisingly, Stone trailed. He was dropped. At one time
Stone's entire vote would have gone to Goebel, but their
agreement, in Stone's view, had been broken. His supporters
would divide almost equally now; and since Hardin and
Goebel stood at almost the same count, the contest would be
very close yet.

On the final, twenty-sixth ballot, crucial areas began to go
for Hardin. Of the first six Stone counties, five went against
Goebel. James gave Crittenden County's vote to Hardin, as
Rhea did for Logan. Bardstown went for Hardin. But in other
towns and urban areas Goebel picked up support—in
Lexington, Louisville, Owensboro, Richmond, Hopkinsville.
Finally the ballot came to Union County, previously for Stone.
With its sixteen votes, Goebel won the nomination. Without
Union he would have lost, for only thirty votes separated the
two contenders at the end.

The nominee appeared before the delegates and in a very
brief speech told them, "I never got anything in my life that
was worth having without a hard fight. . . . I believe the governorship is worth fighting for." Following the talk, Rhea,
Sweeney, James, McCreary, Blackburn, and even Bronston
voiced their support for the party and its choice. As the *New
York Times* noted, the melodrama had ended in a love feast.
Goebel went to the Galt House, ate, and left, as if it were just
another day. He was calm and confident.

All that remained to be done was selection of the other
nominees. The expected choice for lieutenant governor was
J. C. W. Beckham, the young, handsome speaker of the Ken-
tucky house and a proud grandson of a former governor. But
Goebel hesitated to support Beckham, for, as in Louisville and
Covington, two factions struggled in Beckham's hometown of

Bardstown. Ben Johnson, himself a former speaker of the house, had controlled the area's convention vote for Hardin, showing Beckham's political impotence. Finally, however, Goebel went to Beckham.

The nominee for attorney general aided the ticket, for Robert J. Breckinridge, Jr. added the most politically prestigious family name in the commonwealth to the Democratic ranks. As an ex-Confederate he was expected to overcome that group's dissatisfaction with the nominee. (He was, one paper said, "a small bait for the confederate soldier.") A brother of Willie Breckinridge of the *Morning Herald*, Bob Breckinridge had briefly served in the Confederate Congress, and with Goebel in the Kentucky senate. Other candidates included future gubernatorial hopefuls S. W. Hager for treasurer and Harry V. McChesney for superintendent of public instruction. The convention finally was ended.

The goodwill proclaimed was illusory, however. "Mutterings of mutiny or sullen silence" better typified real feelings. The day after the convention closed, Stone placed a "card" in the *Cincinnati Post* in which he told of his agreement with Goebel, arguing that Goebel had pledged to support him in return for a position of power in naming the other candidates and in selection of party leaders. Ex-Congressman W. C. Owens, a Stone manager, indicated to the press that "Goebel betrayed Stone if ever a man was betrayed. He broke his word to him." The statements confirmed the suspicions of disappointed Stone supporters.

Hardin's spokesman, the *Louisville Dispatch*, had ruled out any compromise with Goebel even while the convention met. An editorial proclaimed that "this is no schoolboy game that is now being played in Kentucky. It is genuine political war of the most desperate character." It concluded that Goebel's "revolutionary" methods justified vigorous and "far-reaching" plans of opposition. Hallam, Myers, and Clay opposed the ticket. Breckinridge's *Morning Herald* saw the whole Music Hall affair as a "mob farce," and the platform and candidate but fruits of "a corrupt bargain and political cowardice." And this despite his brother's presence on the ticket. Like the Civil War, Goebelism split families.

Even Watterson's endorsement of Goebel—which required a great deal of political leapfrogging and shuffling of past words—was not strong, as he said the paper was "compelled" to support the ticket. Perhaps he remembered the thousands of dollars lost in 1896 when it had not done so.

The conduct and the proceedings at the Music Hall turned more voters against Goebel than anything had since passage of the Goebel Election Law. But had Goebel not followed the course he did at the convention it is doubtful that he would have received the nomination. Whereas the Election Law had been a tactical error—unless, as enemies charged, it would declare him elected—his conduct at the Music Hall was not. Both would drive voters away from him, but it was vital to win the nomination. Now he could appeal to the people, to the masses that he believed would elect him, and perhaps regain their trust—and votes. To defeat the corporations required his victory at the Music Hall, at almost whatever cost. And he had paid the price of victory.

Goebel told a brother that "the nomination has given me a power that nothing else could have given me; and if I am elected my power will be still further increased. I do not doubt my election." The question was still whether the L & N controlled Kentucky or not. He added, "I have made up my mind not to be beaten, no matter what is done by the L & N. . . . And I shall not take any chances. So far as I can do so, I shall make my election certain."

The Republicans met in relative quiet but not complete harmony. The leading contender for their nomination seemed a weak figure when compared to such talented former candidates as John Marshall Harlan and W. O. Bradley. Yet William Sylvester Taylor did lead. His background contrasted with Goebel's urban origins. Born in 1853 in a Kentucky log cabin near Morgantown, Taylor grew up on a farm in the same general area. Not wealthy, not well educated, he was ambitious, and so he entered politics. Taylor won election in a predominately Democratic county, and he had enough influence by 1888 to be chosen as a delegate to the national convention. He ran with Bradley in 1895 and won the office of attorney general.

In some ways, however, Taylor was not unlike Goebel. He lacked the personal appeal that many political leaders have, and the graces and physique that attract support. An adequate but not graceful speaker, he was warm and probably well meaning; but he was not a man of strong intellect. The ill-fitting clothes, long, shaggy black hair, and bony fingers of "Tom-Tit" Taylor made him an easy figure for ridicule.

Even Taylor's friends saw much truth in the picture the opposition painted. "Hogjaw" Taylor, said one paper, was industrious and ambitious; but beyond that he was "a slouch in his gait, a boor in his manner, and the butt of the entire bar of Kentucky." The editor portrayed a man who knew few social amenities, crowded his way through parties, and kept a Frankfort boardinghouse to earn money for his large family. Taylor, said the Democrats, "is the personification of all the low and degrading in human tendency."

Taylor came to the convention leading, not because of personality, but because of persistence. Since Republicans had expected to lose in 1899, strong candidates abandoned the canvass. Bradley's handling of Spanish-American War problems and general voter reaction to his administration kept them away. Taylor stayed in, built up his own "machine," worked hard at the "grass roots," and gained delegate strength. When the Music Hall proceeding split the Democrats, Republicans suddenly saw excellent opportunities for victory. Hopefuls now worked harder, but it was too late.

Governor Bradley represented the old wing of his party, the group which went back to the postwar days and which had built its base on black voters. Bradley himself had voiced his support for social equality among races. Taylor, from western Kentucky, spoke for the younger, "lily-white" branch of the party, however. He and Senator Deboe sought to widen Republican appeal by disassociating the party from the "stigma" of "black Republicanism." A spirit of Negro proscription had risen in the 1890s throughout the South, and in Kentucky it had resulted in a Separate Coach Act that segregated railroad cars. Beyond that the movement slowed in the commonwealth, and blacks continued to vote. Taylor wanted their votes, but he promised little in return. Bradley opposed Taylor, as did a third group led by Lexington *Leader* editor Sam J. Roberts and powerful Danville lawyer John W. Yerkes. But none could overcome Taylor's early delegate lead.

At the convention at Woodland Auditorium in Lexington, Taylor was made the unanimous selection. Black leaders who had threatened to set up a third party were promised future office and one of their number was made permanent secretary. With that threat seemingly settled, Taylor sought to placate the governor, who refused to attend the convention. Taylor spokesmen offered to make Bradley's nephew Edwin P. Morrow the candidate for secretary of state, if "Billy O. B." would campaign for them. He refused. And so a thirty-year-old superintendent of schools from Knox County in the mountains received that office. A farmer's son and former schoolteacher, Caleb Powers was a rising politician. Educated at Union College, then A&M in Lexington, then West Point (which he had to leave because of poor eyesight), at Northern Indiana Normal School's law department, and finally in a postgraduate course at Centre College, Powers was an intelligent, dignified, shrewd, and sensitive young man. After his wife's death within six months of their marriage, Powers threw himself into politics more vigorously. He grew colder, more reserved, and more determined. By 1899 politics was almost his sole interest.

The Republican ticket, like the Democratic one, was filled for the most part with young men like Powers who represented the new wave of untried leaders swept in by the chaos of the 1890s. As new factions replaced old, politics became almost a question of who could best keep the most elements of the old party while attracting new faces to a coalition.

The race would not be just a two-man affair, however.

Democrats defeated at the Music Hall had corresponded, argued, and then finally agreed to form a third party. At a preliminary meeting some 500 people assembled in Lexington. Among the Democratic ex-congressmen were Willie Breckinridge, W. C. Owens, Phil Thompson, and G. W. Adams. Reformer William Beckner came, as did "Boss" John Whallen. Myers represented his faction, while "Roaring Bill" Sweeney and other defeated candidates for office at the Democratic convention spoke for their causes.

Leadership for this bolters' meeting came from former Governor John Young Brown. His temporary reconciliation with Goebel was no more. Spoken of as a candidate back in 1898 before the Democrats had started their canvass, he had dropped out. According to Goebel, in a letter he wrote to Justus, Brown had then pledged to support him. Now Goebel saw him as another betrayer, another enemy. A good speaker, though somewhat haughty and reticent in private, Brown turned his full fury on the Democratic nominee. After florid references to home, daughters, flowers, the American Revolution, Henry Clay, and Robert E. Lee, he asked, "Has manhood fled to brutish beasts and are we to be called up and voted like dumb driven cattle?" He argued that Goebelism must be defeated by this group, by "real" Democrats. They would "save" the party from the clutches of those who would remove fundamental rights. Anarchists led by Goebel should be destroyed, said Brown. He, for one, would not "bow my neck to the usurpation of the Louisville convention."

Two weeks later a convention of these "bolters" assembled in Lexington. With a one-legged, ex-Confederate soldier sitting as chairman, the delegates chose at least four more ex-Confederates, including P. P. Johnston, among the seven men they nominated for the minor offices. Brown was an easy choice for governor. The earlier leaders were now joined by allies Hallam and Richard Knott—the latter the independent editor of the Louisville *Evening Post*, and a man whose brother served the L & N as vice president. The forces opposing Goebel were growing.

Even expected allies turned against him. Although a relatively insignificant party since the Democrats had taken over their free silver plank, a small group of Populists held their convention, promptly rejected Goebel, and condemned his election law. Goebel observed these damaging developments as he prepared for formal campaigning and the most important speech of his short life.

6

"I ASK NO QUARTER AND I FEAR NO FOE"

THE CAMPAIGN OPENED at the Democratic stronghold of Mayfield on 12 August. Initial speeches traditionally set the tone for the entire race and were widely reprinted. In the period before his speech, when candidates usually mingled with the crowd to shake hands and tell jokes, Goebel was ill at ease, restless, nervous, almost aloof. The irony became evident: whereas Goebel appealed to the masses with his stands on issues, his personality belied that appeal. The contradiction would haunt him as he spoke warmly and with strong feeling about matters that affected and interested the masses; but on a person-to-person basis he moved with a cold, emotionless aura, and he failed to articulate his feelings effectively.

Standing before the crowd as he prepared to give his speech, Goebel personified a type of Kentucky leader seldom seen on the political stage before. For almost from the advent of statehood, politicians of the commonwealth had depended heavily on strong oratory to win votes; they had stressed family ties and common ancestries; and postwar Democrats had emphasized their Confederate ties to prestigious leaders. The northerner Goebel could not make such appeals. Partly Populist, partly Progressive, a strong reformer, yet a powerful machine politician, Goebel was a transitional southern leader. His appeal would be different in that it would be more issue-oriented. This is not to say that Goebel ignored oratory, for he carefully prepared speeches with a good grasp of audience psychology. By repeating phrases and concepts and by using very little figurative language, he could give an effective talk. Perhaps not the demagogue some analysts have presented, Goebel did use some demagogic techniques. But in Kentucky politics that did not make him very different.

The audience he faced had tired of four years of Republican control and they saw Goebel seeking to redeem for the Democracy the office that was rightfully theirs. Uncertain Democrats wanted to be convinced that he was their man. Thus Goebel could have stressed common goals, healed wounds, and skirted divisive issues. But little in Goebel's personality slowed his chosen course of attack. Attacking and fighting made the campaign easier for him. Goebel simply said the things he had been saying since entering politics a dozen years earlier. Only now the audience was not a few senators or a small Covington gathering, but a statewide one, and the stakes were much greater.

Goebel addressed voters who had experienced the greatest railroad rate discrimination, who had suffered most from falling prices. These people knew what Goebel was saying. As Thomas D. Clark noted: "They needed a political Joshua to lead them from the wilderness of Republicanism and railroad abuse into a Jericho of Democracy." Their Joshua was William Goebel. Many Democratic voters, particularly small farmers, followed the path of free silver, railroad regulation, cheaper textbooks, and a return to Democratic control. Goebel aimed at these men when he gave unqualified support to the McChord railroad bill, the Chinn textbook bill, his own Election Law, and Blackburn's return to the senate.

In his speech at Mayfield that hot August day, he began with an almost xenophobic, Populist attack on the L & N, which was owned, he said, by the Belmonts of New York and by English investors. Controlled, concentrated wealth—the L & N monopoly—had sought to select the Democratic nominee, but the people had won out and chosen him. The gold standard, high tariffs, oppressive trusts—these were Republican stands; while Democrats protected the "common man." Goebel demanded decreased state government expenses, lower taxes, and increased school aid. But the issue that transcended others was "whether the trusts or the people shall rule . . . whether the Louisville and Nashville Railroad Company is the servant or the master of the people of this Commonwealth." Unfortunately for Goebel, reaction to his speech was mixed, due in part no doubt to the fact that he had collapsed from heat exhaustion in the middle of it. Blackburn quickly had filled in until Goebel recovered and returned to conclude. But, as campaigns go, this was not an auspicious debut.

Throughout the canvass, Goebel continued the themes stressed in his opening speech. The brunt of his attack fell on railroads. As he once told an acquaintance, "I believe I have a mission to perform," and part of that "mission" was to humble what he saw as a dangerous and greedy force influencing Kentucky politics. Long before Goebel entered politics it had been customary for railroads to contribute to political campaigns, but 1899 brought a difference in scale. August Belmont supposedly said that the line eventually spent a half million dollars to defeat the Democrat. Such moves strengthened Goebel's resolution and determination.

In speeches across the state, Goebel traced his long-standing opposition to the L & N that had begun in his first legislative term: "From that day to this the Louisville and Nashville Railroad Company has regularly camped on my political trail. . . . I have done a little camping myself." He would then tell of his various efforts against the line, including support for moves to limit laborers' working hours and to outlaw "yellow dog" contracts. Privately he told a friend that when elected he would get an indictment against Milton Smith, Basil Duke, and their colleagues, and put them all in jail.

Clearly the L & N could expect no sympathy; they believed they would not even get a fair hearing. Reaction—at times

Great Days for Political Grafters
Louisville Times, September, 1899

extreme reaction—followed. In the view of men like Smith, Goebel was leading a frontal attack on their business, their system, their whole philosophy. If successful, this leader might tear down all that they had spent years building. They could not accept regulation if it promised their future destruction, and they feared "the Kenton King" would use any means to destroy them. Smith, hardly one to retreat, struck back. He asked former allies who had stayed with the Democrats to return the free passes given earlier in the year. Funds went to subsidize newspapers which opposed "Boss Bill." In Louisville especially pressures increased on the railroad workers.

Watterson, writing as "your personal friend," had warned Belmont that the Democrats would be elected, for "under the operation of the Goebel [election] law the result is not left to chance." Belmont should, for expediency, go with the ticket (as Watterson did). But the L & N refused, and Belmont wrote Goebel a letter which the candidate disclosed later to show L & N opposition to him—if that needed to be stressed. "If in order to gain adherents to your political ambition in the State," Belmont wrote, "you endeavor to create a prejudice of the people against the L. and N. railroad, and try to excite animosity and legislation destructive to its interests, the L. and N. railroad is driven to take the best means within the law and its right to meet such attacks, and this it is now doing by bringing before the public the arguments which are at its command to counteract the evil influences of your unjustifiable hostility." The lines were clearly defined. No position of compromise existed.

If the L & N and its supposed excesses concerned Goebel above all, he also made appeals to groups who cared little about that particular issue. Since the 1890s, he had seldom used familiar Democratic routes to victory. Although some party leaders, such as Willie Breckinridge, stressed sectional reconciliation, many others continued to wave their own "bloody shirt" and to cry of "black domination." Goebel never used that ploy. Unlike rising southern demagogues, such as "Pitchfork Ben" Tillman in South Carolina or James K. Vardaman in Mississippi, who wooed agrarian votes with white supremacy appeals, the man from northern Kentucky in fact appealed for black support. In Kentucky, as elsewhere, this appeal was not revolutionary for Democrats, as New Departure leaders had at least voiced such sentiments. And Populists in the state had made a strong but largely unsuccessful effort to win black support. But Goebel did so now on an unprecedented scale. Discerning black dissatisfaction with Taylor, he saw a real possibility that he could woo a sizable black vote.

Goebel's record was acceptable to blacks, for he had not voted on the Separate Coach Act in the senate. Black speakers toured the state for the Democrats, and Negroes in several cities organized Goebel Clubs. Danger existed in this appeal, however. Too close an identification with blacks would antagonize some white voters. Republicans continually pressed Goebel to state his position about the Separate Coach Act. Finally, torn between keeping Democrats in the ranks and only possibly attracting new Negro allies, Goebel declared that he did not favor repeal of the act and would enforce it, if accommodations were in fact equal. This stand, coupled with Taylor's reluctant statement later that he opposed the bill, weakened Goebel's appeal to blacks. Nevertheless, that he had made such a strong appeal underscores Goebel's departure from traditional approaches.

Much as Huey Long would do later, Goebel avoided using the common "Lost Cause" issue with Democratic voters. But then Goebel ventured into a dangerous situation when he even alluded to Confederates. The president of the state Confederate Veterans Association opposed Goebel. Brown Democrats hit hard at Goebel's Unionist background and his "murder" of ex-Confederate Sanford. The *Louisville Dispatch* asked readers, "What husband, if he has the manhood, the chivalry of a gentleman, can look into the innocent and trusting face of his wife and tell her that he voted to elevate to the gubernatorial chair the man whose vile obscenity in the public press sent Sandford [*sic*] to his grave and Sandford's wife to an asylum for the insane?" When Blackburn and other speakers denied that Goebel had written the article, the *Dispatch* gleefully printed a facsimile, in Goebel's handwriting, of the article about "Gonorrhea" John. In this race at least, ex-Confederates, especially among the officer class, might not be safely tucked in the Democratic column. Goebel, of course, had a defense. He pointed to Robert Breckinridge's position on the ticket as an indication of his support for the men of the gray. But overall he could only hope that his other appeals would override this deficit with the party faithful.

He had to have the same hopes on another issue as well. Both Goebel and Brown proclaimed their free silver views in opposition to the Republicans' "sound money" ones. Carlisle then presented his version of Goebel's actions in 1896, when Goebel had pledged to support the gold standard in exchange for Carlisle's support against Hallam. Now the former secretary of the treasury received his revenge for Goebel's turn to free silver at the convention that had followed. He exposed Goebel as a gold man in 1896, and free silver enthusiasts demanded an answer. In reply, Goebel told audiences that he was "proud" to incur Carlisle's wrath and pointed to his own actions later in 1896 as an indication of his stands. He wisely skirted earlier events.

All these matters—the blacks, the Confederates, the gold issue—troubled undecided voters already bothered by Goebel's negative associations with "bossism," the Election Law, and the Music Hall Convention. Goebel's chances for victory had not greatly increased during the campaign. Besides that, any hopes of compromise with the Brown Democrats decreased as their leaders took to the campaign trail. Personal attacks replaced questions of philosophy; and calm, reasonable discussion deserted the canvass almost completely. Former Congressman W. C. Owens told of the betrayal of Stone and the emergence of the *Courier-Journal* as the "avowed champion of fraud, force and duplicity." Carlisle asked "honorable gentlemen everywhere" to form their own opinion "as to the propriety and good faith" of Goebel in the past, as he cited Goebel's "betrayal" in 1896. United States Senator Lindsay opposed "King William I," as did Clay and former Governor Buckner. Judge Beckner, a reformer at the constitutional convention, refused to aid the regular Democrats, citing the fraudulent "rump" convention that had nominated Goebel. "Goebelism" used the "most unblushing corruption" to achieve its aims, he asserted, and every vote cast for its leader "would encourage our young men to believe that straight methods do not bring honor in Kentucky." Bronston spoke at the Opera House in Lexington and told of the "cold-blooded, selfish ambition" of Goebel. He described the "humiliating and despicable methods" used to pass the election law, and told how his former senate colleague had "proved false to those instincts which characterize true manhood." Neither Hardin nor Stone gave Goebel active support. Even prominent Democrats outside the state joined the attack, among them former Illinois Governor John Peter Altgeld, the arch-villain of conservatives because of his pardon of the Haymarket rioters. Goebel faced an angry, diverse, and articulate opposition.

More important, influential newspapers spread the Brown Democrats' message. In Louisville Richard Knott's *Evening Post* joined the *Dispatch* in an editorial effort to defeat "Boss Bill." The latter paper became particularly crucial to the "Brownies," as the L & N distributed it free across the state. Appealing chiefly to Democrats, the *Louisville Dispatch* strongly opposed the Republicans and the gold standard. It reprinted the *Courier-Journal*'s earlier words of censure for both free silver and Goebel, and noted the contradictions in the paper's position. Editorials and news stories stressed the Sanford affair in sensational terms. But the chief target remained Goebel—"a political desperado of the most desperate character." His Election Law sought to create an oligarchy, said the *Dispatch*, and "murdered" any thoughts of home rule.

Caustic Willie Breckinridge of the Lexington *Morning Herald* denounced Goebel in a biting vein. "The better class of Democrats" in the South oppose such election laws, said the aristocratic editor, who noted of Goebel himself: "A gentleman cannot be made out of a vulgarian." The candidate's furious attacks on railroads were but "irrelevant hellabaloo" against a straw man. This "demagoguery of the clamor against corporations" by a "most expert political schemer, trickster and charlatan" must not be allowed to succeed. The "infectious, festering disease" of Goebelism cannot continue, or it would destroy Kentucky. Tell us about the Sanford assassination. Read us the Stone agreement. Explain your gold stance in 1896, taunted the old ex-Confederate.

It was left to Hallam, another ex-Confederate, to inject one of the few light moments into a serious campaign devoid of humor. Even before Goebel had taken the field, Hallam had given a talk at Bowling Green. From the audience a partisan Goebel heckler rose and yelled, "Didn't you say in the Louisville convention, not four weeks ago, that if the Democrats of Kentucky . . . nominated a yaller dog for governor, you'd vote for 'im?"

"I did," answered the speaker.

How could he now oppose Goebel, then?

Waiting for absolute quiet, the witty Hallam replied that he did in fact say he would support the Democratic nominee even if a "yaller dog."

"But, he added, *"lower than that ye shall not drag me!"*

Goebel and his partisans did not accept such attacks without rebuttal, and in some cases they caused the harsh words themselves. Papers which supported Goebel, such as the *Glasgow Times*, countered by stressing the corruption of these "professional purificationists" who called themselves "the Honest Election League." "Boss" Whallen "wouldn't know a political principle if he met [it] in the road"; Breckinridge, Owens, and Beckner were without a Democratic bone in their bodies, said the editor. The *Courier-Journal* printed huge cartoons tying the L & N to Brown and showing Smith and Belmont distributing money to defeat Goebel. The newspaper ridiculed the "holier-than-thou, Louisville and Nashville political brakemen and moral conductors" led by Basil Duke.

The Democratic nominee did not let his supporters fight alone. In late August Goebel made his own Bowling Green speech and called Hallam "a drunkard and debauchee," who had the face of "a cancerous beefsteak." While calling Duke "a professional corruptionist" later, he linked Myers to lottery money, Owens to gambling, and Breckinridge to the scandal that had ended his political career. This attack and others brought opponents to intensify their campaign and removed the few restraints on them. Duke portrayed Goebel as "liar, a slanderer and an assassin"; and others used even harsher words. As in the past, Goebel still evoked bitter reaction and excited violent emotions. He had stated the terms of battle well when he cried out: "I ask no quarter and I fear no foe."

On 22 August 1899, a festive and almost victorious spirit prevailed in a small town in eastern Kentucky. London sat in the citadel of state Republicanism and there the party chose to open the campaign. Republicans were confident, yet worried—confident that Goebel was the weakest of the three possible Democratic candidates and that their opposition was divided, but worried because Goebel was so different and his methods were so unpredictable. In a fight between the forces of good and of the Devil, people should, they reasoned, readily support the morally right one—but if they somehow did not, or if Goebel used fraud to win, then his weakness, as they saw it, would become a strength. They would be destroyed. In the thirty or more years before, no opponent had aroused such intense Republican hatred as Goebel did.

Taylor opened his campaign before a large, friendly audience. In a 2½-hour talk, he stressed his support for the national administration, defended the state one, and focused chiefly on Goebel. Since slavery had never flourished in the mountains, said the nominee, it was fitting to open this struggle to maintain liberty in the shadow of the mountains. Taylor warned the crowd to organize and demand a fair election: "This is your only salvation. If it fails you then the deadly coils of tyranny will tighten about you and crush to death your political liberties." A month later, Republicans continued to stress the same themes, though the desperate character of the opposition was accented even more. A government "of force and fraud" was about to be established, if Democrats won. They would rob the ballot box and end republican government. The voter, Taylor cautioned, must act, for if "Goebelism" became entrenched in the state, all would be lost. "Now is the last opportunity."

In their appeals all three groups increased the dangers of discord after the election. By portraying its cause as unfailingly correct, and the others' as utterly wrong, each side strengthened its followers' resolve to resist an unfavorable decision. Goebel suggested that his defeat would result in an absolutely corrupt government controlled by corporate wealth; Brown and Taylor stressed that their defeat would bring a dictator to power and destroy representative government. The problem with such appeals was obvious. What did you do if the opposition did win? Could such an expected evil be tolerated, even if honorably chosen? And what would happen if the race was so close that fraud was suspected? Still the vitriolic oratory and caustic editorials continued as the campaign drew to an end, for the leaders realized that the race would be very close.

To the Democratic nominee, his campaign seemed to be faltering. He had not gained a great deal of additional support, and certainly he had not brought factional enemies back to the party. It probably would have been a fairly easy Democratic year, had Goebel not been the nominee; the Republicans had thought so at least. But this Democrat had many handicaps to overcome: his immigrant "foreign" background, his non-aristocratic family, his scorn for established methods, his "boss" reputation, his shooting of Sanford, his stand on free silver, his alienation of ex-Confederates, his Election Law, his conduct at the Music Hall, his approach, his very personality.

In danger of losing support and short on funds, Goebel turned to the one national candidate who was now most popular with the Kentucky Democracy. William Jennings Bryan, still the "boy orator of the Platte," had spurned initial party efforts to bring him to Kentucky. According to Urey Woodson, the "Great Commoner" believed Goebel was probably illegally selected, and in a meeting of the two the Kentuckian's language had supposedly offended Bryan. But the defeated candidate of 1896 still sought the presidency, and a Demo-

The Kentucky Political Situation
Washington Post, October 19, 1899

cratic administration might be able to reverse the 281 votes that had cost him the state earlier. Ambition helped bring Bryan to Goebel.

The two began their whirlwind railroad campaign in western Kentucky in mid-October. On the first day Bryan made ten speeches, reaching an estimated 25,000 voters; he emphasized party loyalty. He appealed particularly to the agrarians, asking them to support the Democrats. In other areas he asked blacks to abandon the party of imperialism for the Democrats. By the time the train reached Covington an estimated 150,000 had heard the two men speak over a three-day period. Bryan had repaired a faltering candidacy and, as Woodson (who accompanied them) remembered, "Goebel's friends were wild with enthusiasm." A writer in the *Kentucky Gazette* proclaimed, "There seems to be little doubt of his election now."

Such a situation did not help the Republican campaign, which had had its problems as well. The estimated 65,000 black voters had shown little enthusiasm for Taylor, although his reluctant support for repeal of the Separate Coach Act helped some. The endorsement of the Committee of the General Association of Negro Baptists proved useful, but not decisive. The *Courier-Journal*'s comment that "the Taylor canvass recalls the remark about the man who was winking at a pretty girl in the dark. He knew what he was doing but nobody else did," did not exaggerate that much.

And, perhaps more important, Republicans had not healed their own factional wounds. Bradley initially refused to campaign for Taylor. Then came the unexpected announcement that the governor would speak in Louisville—the day after Bryan left the state. A large crowd gathered, including many blacks. Bradley appealed to the Negroes, citing his appointments of four blacks to somewhat minor state positions. Democrats had enacted railroad segregation in the state, he told them. Would you vote for them? "I have never been ashamed of being the friend of the negro, . . ." he declared, and "I have never been afraid of the bugbear 'social equality.' " He and the Republicans supported justice for "an unfortunate race." This attempt to hold Republican voters coincided with an appeal to Brown Democrats, whose nominee was ill and virtually unable to campaign. Bradley praised the "bolters" and their leaders, stressing how the "better men" among Democrats refused to support Goebel. Then, having said nothing about the Republican nominee, "Billy O. B." ended with, "And go to the polls and elect Taylor." As the wild cheering went on, Louisville Republican leader and former partner of John Marshall Harlan, Augustus E. Willson turned to Bradley and said, "That's the slickest thing you ever did in your life."

Watterson's paper coyly suggested that Bradley's sudden reversal was due to Taylor's promise to support his expected candidacy for the senate. But for whatever reason, Bradley toured the state for his new friend "Bill" Taylor, and even the *Courier-Journal* admitted that the governor's eloquent talks were "the equal of any Republican speech heard in any Kentucky campaign for a long time." Republicans had successfully met the challenge posed by Bryan's speeches, and had strengthened their chances for a final victory.

As the long campaign neared an end, all three parties turned to the crucial areas. With the east safely Republican by large margins, and the west Democratic by more uncertain ones, the central and northern areas held the keys— particularly Louisville. It was no accident that Bradley had spoken there first, for in Louisville the "Brownies" had their strongest support. Republicans wanted to carry the county as they had four years before. When the influential *Irish-American* criticized Goebel for his "insinuations, epithets and threats against gentlemen" and "treachery and slander of his friends," Republican hopes increased. Goebel spent a large part of the last three weeks in the Falls City countering these appeals. In one speech before a predominately German audience, he began in his original language. On another occasion he spoke in a working class neighborhood and pledged full support for laborers who struck for higher wages. At every opportunity Goebel defended the Election Law and the Music Hall, praised the McChord and Chinn bills, damned the "bossism" of the "corrupt" L & N trust, and reviewed his own record on reform issues. And when he said, "I didn't know whether it was safe for me to come to the city of Louisville or not," laughter followed.

But it was a serious time, and Goebel's merriment masked real threats. Both sides predicted and expected violence and fraud. Both viewed the opposition in the most derogatory way possible. In Louisville, Brown Democrats backed by Whallen remembered the conduct of the primary in that city only months before. The *Dispatch* suggested that citizens band together to prevent fraud this time, but added, "if there must be a row let it be started by the Goebelites." A Republican speaker warned, with figurative noose in hand, that if the Democrats attempted to steal the election, "We will decorate the Williamsburg bridge with ornaments never dreamed of by an architect."

Speaking in the Louisville Music Hall in his last speech before election day, Blackburn combined threats and compromises when he emphasized that "they have thrown down the gauntlet, we accept the challenge. We will win all or lose all. . . . I counsel no violence; but we want the people to know their rights and to maintain them." Louisville's mayor, a Goebel supporter, proclaimed that with rumors of "riot and bloodshed" so prevalent, he would take any measures to insure a peaceful vote. On election day he swore in almost 300 private police to patrol the polls. The day before that his Jefferson County election board had dismissed Republican election officials from half of the precincts and replaced them with less partisan ones.

To the opposition all this meant that Goebelites would attempt to repeat the earlier primary maneuvers in Louisville. Governor Bradley consulted with Knott, Duke, and the editor of the *Louisville Dispatch*, and ordered the militia made ready should violence break out. On election day each side had armed men in readiness—Bradley's militia and the mayor's private police. The press for each group proclaimed "Bayonet Rule" and accused the other of intimidation as election day began.

Surprisingly, the election passed quietly in most Kentucky cities. There were disruptions and fights, but compared to most state elections all went very well. In Louisville some of the militia marched out into the streets once late in the day, did virtually nothing, and paraded back. Even the *Courier-Journal* admitted that all was unexpectedly calm there.

That evening when Watterson joined Blackburn and Goebel for dinner at the Seelbach Hotel, William Goebel's political astuteness was evident. Two old enemies sat with the young intruder they had once hated. Their aid might now make him governor. But did he have voter support? The three men dined and awaited the electorate's answer.

7

"FORCE WILL BE MET
WITH FORCE"

GOD REIGNS and the Government in Frankfort Still Lives," proclaimed a Republican headline as the first returns came in. The Democrat had lost. More cautiously and accurately, the *Courier-Journal* predicted, "Slow Returns and Close Finish." The worst had happened: an extremely narrow margin separated Taylor and Goebel. In a year that should have been Democratic, that party's nominee had barely tied the Republican, if that.

The apparent closeness of the vote reflected in part the Democratic candidate's weakness in the agrarian, Populist, western part of the state, where Goebel failed to gain expected majorities. Except for heavily black-populated Christian County, Goebel's percentage of the Democratic vote dropped beneath Bryan's 1896 figures in every single county west of Louisville. The insignificant Populist party's attacks on the Goebel law apparently reflected western agrarian dislike for "Boss Bill." This area also had been one of the centers of Confederate strength.

Another area of expected support—the urban centers—followed a more mixed pattern. In Ashland, Covington, Newport, and Louisville along the Ohio, and in Frankfort, Lexington, and other Bluegrass cities, Goebel increased Bryan's dismal percentage of 1896. In the west he did not. Of the

The Political Tug of War
Indianapolis News, November 15, 1899

counties that contained the ten largest urban areas of the commonwealth, Goebel carried seven, but he had needed to do even better if he wanted a safe margin of victory. Democrats had reason for concern.

Republicans, on the other hand, were sanguine. Taylor had been able to retain the usual percentage of the mountain vote, while his "lily white" branch had done very well in western Kentucky, his home area. But Taylor had not swept the state either, chiefly because of the urban vote. Although Goebel had not been as successful in all the cities as he had hoped, he had increased Democratic majorities in the eastern ones. And a shift of one percentage of the vote of urban centers meant many more ballots for the Democrats than a similar shift would in isolated, underpopulated counties. The close results meant that each vote gained added significance, that every local board had a more vital role, and that the State Board of Election Commissioners—as Republicans feared—would give the final decision.

With the outcome in doubt a month before the board met, the Republicans and the badly defeated Brown Democrats joined in dire predictions that fraud would overcome their rightful majority. Three days after the election the *Louisville Dispatch* warned that Goebel would not accept the legitimate results and would risk civil war: "He must be met by bold measures." The same issue of the *Evening Post* told of a mass meeting at the now infamous Music Hall, where editor Knott had asked citizens to "stop the steal" of the governorship. That day a protest in Lexington's Opera House attracted Bronston and Breckinridge. Resolutions were passed in support of Bradley's use of the militia, and the "silver-tongued orator" even suggested that force should be used to resist turning over the governor's seat to Goebel. In an editorial a few days later he wrote of "this unholy and wicked attempt to feloniously steal the governorship." The opposition expected Goebel's election board to do its work well.

Meanwhile Democratic papers began telling of Republican "fraud" in the election itself. In Nelson County, where ballots bore the name "W. P." Taylor rather than the correct

"W. S.," the local board threw out these Republican votes. That decision did not stand, however. Less than a week after the election, the *Courier-Journal* printed a story telling how thin "tissue" ballots had been used in the mountains. This action supposedly enabled Republicans to see whether their employees voted as expected. (Actually both parties had used these ballots.) In Johnson County, Democrats declared these ballots illegal and challenged them. That party's supporters in Louisville asked that the entire city and county vote—carried by Taylor—be thrown out because of Bradley's use of the militia.

The Republicans grew less confident about their chances. Goebel and his lawless followers were marching toward "the ultimate crime"—stealing the election—said party leaders, and he had to be stopped. Bradley wrote President McKinley of the "revolution" in the commonwealth. "I fear," said the governor, "that I may not be able to crush the spirit of lawlessness and preserve the peace." He asked that 1,000 regular army soldiers be sent to Fort Thomas, and that the state militia be given blankets, 890 rifles, and 50,000 rounds of ammunition. Whether this request was met or not, promised Bradley, "I will not surrender to a lawless mob." McKinley, a political rival in national affairs, did not send the soldiers.

In the mountains, the fury of an isolated, partisan people brought forth bitter resolutions. Caleb Powers's Knox County Republicans pledged their lives "to resist such awful encroachment on our most sacred rights." Taylor would be given his rightful office "by peaceable means if we can, by forcible ones if we must." In Rockcastle County a similar theme emerged against this "vicious serpent," this "monster" and "usurper." Republicans there declared that "before this ring of looters shall deprive us of the victory we have won in this contest, we will shoulder our guns and march to the music of war."

More cautious Republicans and anti-Goebel Democrats realized the dangers of this explosive atmosphere. Breckinridge in the *Morning Herald* noted that "thoughtful men are alarmed at the possibility of bloodshed." Compromise, or at least a conference of the principals, was needed. But neither side could do that. The Republican leadership had splintered following its brief election unity, as Bradley quarreled with Taylor, while Caleb Powers now led a more outspoken and forceful wing that would resist Goebel to the end. Brown Democrats and Goebel Democrats remained the bitterest of enemies, and the personality of William Goebel made the opposition shun any compromise. The outcome would be left to the election board, then, and it came under the most intense pressure.

The local county boards had already sent their returns to Frankfort. And, although newspapers differed on the results, it seemed certain that the Republicans had a plurality. Republicans pointed out that this came about even though the opposition controlled the polls, the counting, and the certifying. Local boards had altered votes, they charged, but still could not overcome Taylor's large lead over Goebel. Democratic hopes lay in their appeal that Jefferson County's vote, and votes of the mountain counties where "tissue" ballots had been used, should not be counted because of fraud and illegal force. If the election board refused to allow these ballots, then Goebel would win.

Amid rumors of how Republicans were turning the state militia into a partisan army; with stories circulating that Bradley had stated he would refuse to leave office should Goebel be declared elected; and while the national press ridiculed and criticized the commonwealth's actions, the board prepared to meet.

The *Courier-Journal* pledged to accept their decision: "If the Republicans are declared the victors, nobody will block their way to Frankfort." Several Democratic leaders told reporters that Goebel would not contest election board decisions. On 2 December, just days before the board met, Watterson, speaking for his party, said that they would submit to the decision, whatever it was. Democrats expected a favorable result. Two commissioners—Ellis and Pryor—had given speeches for Goebel during the campaign, while Poyntz had been among the candidate's strongest supporters. All owed their selection to William Goebel. All had been strong partisans. Not unexpectedly, the Republicans predicted an unfavorable decision.

A few weeks earlier, when Democratic commissioners in Johnson County had started to invalidate that county's vote because of the supposed "illegal" ballots, angry Republicans gathered as they met. The Democrats, said one Republican observer, found a town filled with men "standin' around like they was goin' to a funeral, and indeed, the Commissioners believed there might be one." They did not change the results. Desperate Republicans now tried a similar ploy as the state board met. Certain in their own minds that their rightful victory would be stolen unless they acted, the party leaders gambled. In doing so they made the first move toward their fatal error.

The board convened, and on 4 December 1899—court day—hundreds of Republicans gathered in Frankfort. Taylor had advised party leaders to send men to the city, so that their presence, he later stated, would "exercise a moral influence on [the] contest." On Sunday a group of fifty arrived, and the Democrats promptly labeled them "the advance guard of the army of intimidationists." The next day the numbers approached 500, according to one estimate. Watterson's paper noted that the L & N had brought them without charge. In an interview later Smith declared that as "a simple matter of business" the train had been secured by Republicans for a $1,000 fee.

Guns were prominently displayed by the observers, whom Republicans weakly defended as citizens only there to demonstrate for their rights. Leaders apparently believed that in the atmosphere created the board would feel compelled to issue a fair decision; Democrats saw it as only another attempt by Republicans to use force to influence a vote. After hearing arguments for three days in these conditions, the commissioners adjourned and issued their decision on Saturday, 9 December.

Former Justice Pryor of the Court of Appeals joined Ellis in a two-to-one majority that declared Taylor governor. Goebel had overlooked only one thing in his scheme to gain power, said critics—the possibility that the commissioners might be honest. The majority of the board—Poyntz dissented—emphasized that the law gave them no legal power to go behind the official county returns; they thus must be recognized. The board did unofficially state later that if they had such powers they would declare the Louisville vote illegal, due to militia involvement. That meant nothing, however, since their official actions gave the final count: Taylor, 193,714; Goebel 191,331; Brown, 12,140; and Populist John Blair, 2,936. Certificates of election were issued, and three days later Kentucky's second Republican governor was inaugurated.

Despite Republican expectations and previous Democratic assurances, the contest had not ended, however. The Democratic State Central, Executive, and Campaign committees gathered in Frankfort on the fourteenth. Their party had one last possible appeal. Ironically, the election bill as introduced originally by Goebel had not contained the provision, later added in committee, that allowed the legislature to be the final judge of the governor's and lieutenant governor's races. With roughly a two-to-one Democratic majority in the newly formed senate and a 58-42 margin for the party in the house, such an appeal had its merits.

Led by Blackburn, with most of the new leaders present, the Democrats decided to contest the election. A confident William told his brother, "No matter what happens, if I live, I shall control the next state convention, and through it the State organization, which will hold power." If not selected governor this year, he would be elected senator in 1901. He did not fear for his political future.

Watterson evaluated the Democratic decision to contest the election as "A Brave Venture"; Republicans submerged in a legislative minority did not see the move in such a courageous light. Other opposition actions did not change that view. The Goebel Election Law allowed the board to judge all cases involving the other elective offices. Thus while the legislature heard evidence on the two top offices, the board would be deciding the minor races. With Ellis and Pryor still sitting, the results probably would have been the same—a Republican victory. But under increasing pressure, with Democrats angered at their earlier decision, both men resigned.

Taylor named two of his allies as replacements, citing his constitutional power to fill vacant appointive offices; Democrat Poyntz chose another man; and the two selected a third. They cited a provision in the election law giving that power to the commission, if the legislature was not in session. The two Poyntz appointees were strong Goebel Democrats; the Taylor ones were equally favorable to Taylor's cause. Neither side yielded and the Court of Appeals by a partisan 4-3 vote later gave their judicial approval to the three Democrats. Having failed once, the board would not select Republicans next time.

All these efforts had been concluded as the Democratic caucus met on 1 January 1900, just before the legislature began. House Democrats reflected their party's differences, as it took thirteen ballots to select South Trimble, not Goebel's choice, as their nominee for speaker. Senators voted Goebel once again as their candidate for president pro tem, even though they would be involved in deciding whether he was governor. Goebel nominated Blackburn as the caucus choice for United States senator, and the move was unanimously adopted.

But a more dramatic event overshadowed the caucus. A newly elected state senator, Dr. S. B. Harrel of Logan County, strode to the front of the gathering and held aloft two keys. With a good eye for the effect this produced, he charged that "Boss" Whallen had offered him $4500 to vote for Taylor when the time came. This money, he told pleased listeners, was now in a safety-deposit box in a Louisville bank. The keys would prove his charge of bribery. A grand jury ordered the box sealed, and upon opening it, they found the sum Harrel said was there. Since widespread rumors had already told of bribery attempts by both sides, this seemed clear proof. The vaultkeeper swore that Whallen and Harrel had rented the box jointly. Democrats made full use of the case to pressure undecided legislators.

Whallen engaged "Wat" Hardin and Hallam to defend him, and they began by going on the offensive. In a sworn affidavit

Whallen charged Harrel with taking money under false pretenses. According to the owner of "The Buck," Harrel told him that he opposed Goebel; but had been given assurances of $1,000 and promised later appointment as superintendent of a lunatic asylum if he would support the Democrat. He proposed that for enough money to live "without pecuniary loss," he would publically tell all. Whallen then gave Harrel $5,000, said the affidavit, to allow him "to act according to what he represented to be the true dictates of his conscience."

A Franklin grand jury indicted Whallen and a cohort, but when the trial began the defense produced its own answer to Harrel's caucus dramatics. Whallen introduced a paper signed by him, Harrel, and a third party, and witnessed by two others, which contained the agreement Whallen had attested: for $5,000 the state senator would reveal Goebel's "bribery" attempt. Harrel denounced this document as a forgery. Significantly, neither party pursued its case against the other with much fervor after that. Later both cases were dropped. The entire clumsy affair did not turn out as some Democrats backing Harrel had hoped, and his fame faded. Whallen, even if his version was correct, had only met bribery with bribery; and his none too lofty standing did not rise further. Neither man had shown much honor. Overall the trials produced no conclusive result, but—more important—they gave the rumors of bribery a firmer base. Those who wanted to believe the worst about their opposition found supporting evidence in the Whallen-Harrel affair.

The bribery case, despite its sensational aspects, yielded to the legislative actions for first place in public attention, however. The General Assembly convened on 2 January 1900, quickly voted in Goebel and Trimble as leaders of the two houses, and then heard Taylor's message. The governor made virtually a campaign speech against Goebel, warning that the choice was between a future of glorious progress or one darkened by "civil and commercial oppression."

As soon as the message was read a "Notice of Contest" was filed for the offices of governor and lieutenant governor. Goebel charged that illegal ballots had been used in forty counties—the list had grown—and asked that "said election in all of said counties [be] rendered void." A second ground for contest, said the president pro tem, was the conduct of the Louisville election. And thousands of ballots in eight other counties should be voided because, charged Goebel, the L & N had bought votes and threatened employees if they failed to follow the railroad's wishes. In two other counties, continued the Notice of Contest, "duress and open threats" had been used to force election commissioners to sign fraudulent returns. At the meeting of the State Board of Election Commissioners, "a conspiracy was formed" by the L & N and its agent John Whallen. Their "desperate armed men" again influenced the results. All these fraudulent actions should invalidate thousands of ballots, and William Goebel should be declared governor as a result.

The next day each house met to select by lot eleven members to sit as a committee to hear evidence on the gubernatorial contest. The senate journal laconically records the procedure: "The names of the Senators present were written on separate pieces of paper, rolled and placed in a box by the clerk . . . who, after the same had been well shaken, drew the names of three Senators therefrom, separately." None of the three was a Republican. In the house the same method produced surprisingly similar results: seven Democrats and one Republican. The joint committee to decide the governorship would be nine Democrats, one Republican, and one Populist, who usually voted Democratic, while the committee on the lieutenant governor's election was nine-to-two Democratic. Republicans had expected four or five representatives on each. The *Courier-Journal* reported that the majority party was "greatly elated" over the results.

And well they might be, for the odds on such a ratio occurring by chance in the governor's contest are roughly one in fifty (Powers erroneously calculated the odds as much higher). Republicans charged fraud, but they were mystified about how it had been done. Only Democrats had examined the box and had seen the slips, and Republicans were certain that chance had not dictated the unfavorable ratio. Perhaps they were wrong. But another answer comes from a Democrat who wrote a history of his party some years later. According to his version, he had been told "by the official who claims he manipulated the drawing in the House, exactly how he accomplished what he seemed then and seems yet to think was a justified fraud." Unfortunately he does not reveal the method used. Republicans at the time presented a theory that the Democratic clerk rolled Republican names in a tighter roll than Democratic ones. As a result, when the box was shaken, these names filtered to the bottom, allowing the clerk to draw out the Democratic names remaining on top. Another suggested that no matter what slip was drawn, the speaker simply called out a Democrat's name. Other possibilities were advanced. Nothing could be proven. Perhaps it had only been chance.

Before the committees met other business took place. On 10 January Blackburn easily defeated Bradley for United States senator in the joint session. "Old Jo's" alliance with Goebel had brought him the desired prize. Bryan returned and gave a talk praising the new senator.

Then on 15 January, the contest committee began to hear evidence on the governor's race. While several prominent lawyers represented the Democrats, they were overshadowed by the Republican counsel, which included independent Willie Breckinridge and Republican W. O. Bradley. Meeting for most of the time in the ballroom of the Capitol Hotel, the contest committee quickly rejected several of Taylor's key contentions. Republicans charged star-chamber methods, as Democrats produced their witnesses. Each could make a good case for the other's fraud. Neither Republican nor Democrat had conducted a "pure" election.

Committee hearings went on. The relative calm of their deliberations contrasted with the increasing tensions outside. A violent era had existed in Kentucky for decades. "Regulators" and Ku Kluxers after the war, an assassination of a Court of Appeals justice in 1879, such affairs as the Hatfield-McCoy feud of Pike County, the French-Eversole feud in Perry County, the White-Baker feud in Clay County, and the

Logan-Tolliver feud in Rowan County, made the era's bloody reputation a deserved one. Violence was not confined to the mountains either, for the state's overall murder rate by 1890 stood second highest in the nation. To Americans the image of the Kentuckian was increasingly that of a bloody, lawless mountaineer or of a white-frocked, hot-tempered gentleman planter with pistol in hand. Actions in Frankfort the last two weeks of January confirmed such impressions.

Violence first exploded on 16 January at the Capitol Hotel in an incident unrelated to the Goebel contest. Two bitter personal enemies, ex-Congressman David G. Colson and young Lieutenant Ethelbert Scott, quarreled and drew their weapons in the hotel lobby. Both fired at the same time. Scott pulled a bystander in front of him for protection. Colson emptied both of his pistols, while Scott did the same with one. The bystander was killed. Scott was hit four times, and as he fell trying to escape, Colson shot him three more times. Eighteen shots had been fired in less than two minutes and three men, including Scott, had been killed. Four more had been wounded. Colson, also wounded, was arrested. No conviction followed. This event should have warned observers of the dangerous temper that existed in the city. Guns were prevalent and, as the conclusion of the long and bitter political contest neared, solving disputes relied more on force than on law.

Actions by Democratic and Republican partisans had continued to divide the two antagonistic camps. As had happened in the past, the senate stripped Republican Lieutenant Governor John Marshall of his powers. That left Goebel in control of one of the two houses that would decide his fate. Republicans expected an unfavorable decision by the contest committee, but the final vote would be in the entire General Assembly. They hoped enough Democrats would join them to defeat Goebel. That possibility made each vote more crucial, and both parties contested any close races. Up to twenty seats were thus uncertain, with the possibility that half might go to Democrats. Men's memories harkened to the 112 ballots in the recent senatorial race. Would that again occur?

As a rule, though, Republicans expected Goebel to control his party and their legislative votes. Many felt as Breckinridge did. He told his daughter of the "sham trial where I know the decision has been made for weeks and we are only 'playing' a trial." The Republican *Louisville Commercial* proclaimed, as the contest committee neared the end of its deliberations, "Goebel Garrote Tightened." Some desperate Republicans sought to influence the decision in the same way as they had others. Earlier in Johnson County partisans had demonstrated for their cause, and the results favored them. When the election commission had met in December a similar tactic, to Republican eyes, had yielded a similar result. Once again some of the party leaders resorted to this avowedly dangerous stratagem. Taylor and Secretary of State Powers agreed to call Republicans to Frankfort on 25 January.

Courier-Journal headlines told the Democratic reaction to the move: "ARMED MOB OF MOUNTAINEERS Invade Frankfort to Bully the Legislature." "Threats of Assassination," cried out the *Kentucky Gazette*. Over 1,000 men, the majority from eastern Kentucky, had entered the city almost overnight. Most stacked their rifles in the commissioner of agriculture's office, but they retained handguns. The administration supplied the "army" with ham, bread, and coffee. Democratic advocates armed now, if they had not already, and prepared for an outbreak of violence. Poorly housed, sometimes resorting to drink to relieve boredom, the determined men from the mountains milled in the town, as if awaiting orders. On the evening of the day they arrived most of the men left.

Anti-Goebel spokesmen tried to defend the administration's actions by stressing that these law-abiding citizens had only sought to protest the "crime" Goebel sought to perpetrate. The Lexington *Morning Herald* praised the "order and commendable self-restraint" of the protesters. Some Republican newspapers cautiously supported the move. But the overall reaction, even among Republicans, was negative. As Taylor's counsel before the contest committee, W. C. P. Breckinridge, despite his paper's public stand, stood firmly against the bringing of "irresponsible armed men" to Frankfort. He had advised, "in unmeasured terms," that they be withdrawn. Other leaders gave Taylor the same advice. The return of all but 300 of the men lessened criticism, but did not stop it.

The danger of a bloody outbreak continued. Powers remarked on the 29th, "I would a thousand times rather we would fight and be free than to submit and be slaves." His spirit typified others who refused to yield to the evils of "the Kenton King." Large groups of armed men from both parties stood ready for the expected outbreak. The contest committee would make its recommendation shortly. In early February the election commission would begin its deliberations on the minor state offices. By the end of that month the Goebel Democrats, now hated more than ever by Republicans, might well control the state.

Could either side peacefully accept an unfavorable decision after such a long fight? A writer in *Harper's Weekly* predicted "that there will be razors in the air, and that Reason will retire to the cellar and Discretion will hide under the bed." Less figuratively, Breckinridge's *Morning Herald* warned that if the legislature followed their "unconstitutional" course, then "violence and bloodshed" might result. "Force," it predicted, "will be met with force."

8

"LOYAL TO THE GREAT COMMON PEOPLE"

O<small>N THE COLD</small> Tuesday morning of 30 January 1900—despite the many rumored threats to his safety circulating around Frankfort—Goebel did not alter his routine. Coming from his room in the Capitol Hotel, he joined his allies and virtual bodyguards Eph Lillard, warden of the penitentiary, and Jack P. "Dirk Knife" Chinn. The three started for the Capitol building a few blocks away.

As they entered the Capitol grounds the men mentioned how unexpectedly clear the area was, and they wondered aloud if any more "mountaineers" would be arriving. Lillard then moved ahead to make certain that the Capitol interior was safe, for trouble, if it came, was expected to occur there. Chinn, a rather heavyset man, lagged behind Goebel by a few feet. Just as Lillard reached the Capitol at about 11:15, he heard the report of a rifle. He quickly turned around.

Goebel had been shot. More muffled shots were heard. Chinn rushed up, exclaiming, "Goebel, they have killed you." As Goebel sought to rise, Chinn told him to lie down, or "they will shoot you again."

"That's right," he weakly answered.

The momentary quiet was broken as excited legislators hurried out, and a hastily organized group of bystanders began to

Shooting of State Senator William Goebel
Harper's Weekly

carry the wounded man back to the hotel, about five minutes away.

Cries of "Goebel has been shot" quickly spread through the town. The streets filled with onlookers, some carrying rifles and pistols. Angry Democrats talked of revenge and the danger of a mob seemed very real. Then in a surprisingly—and to Democrats, suspiciously—quick action, the militia formed around the state building from where the shots came. Within twenty minutes after the shooting, Republicans were protected from a vengeful crowd.

In the hotel, a doctor examined the wounded man. The crush of observers threatened to disrupt his work, so some were ordered out, and windows were broken to let air in. Goebel lay "white as a sheet," almost bloodless, his pulse weak, his skin cold, his body in shock. The bullet had entered three inches to the right and a half inch above the nipple, shattered a rib, sent bone splinters into one lung, pierced the right lung, and exited through the back near the vertebrae. In an attempt to repair the "quite profuse" bleeding, the physician dressed the wound, began a saline solution, and gave Goebel some opiates. Other doctors quickly offered assistance. Most did not expect Goebel to live through the night. But Goebel thought otherwise, and Arthur wired Justus in the West, "William shot from third floor of state house. Says himself he will recover."

Taylor and four other men, including Breckinridge, had been together in the governor's office in the building from where the shot was fired. Amid the confusion and excitement, Taylor rushed out of the office, revolver in hand for protection. Then, on hearing the news of the event, the governor sadly declared, "It is the act of another Guiteau [President Garfield's assassin]. It is terrible." After quickly conferring with Bradley and Breckinridge, he ordered out the militia— and became a virtual prisoner for the immediate future. Republicans prepared to defend the building should it come under Democratic attack.

The contest committees met that afternoon. Taylor's attorneys asked that further deliberations be suspended, or at least postponed until quieter times. After being refused this request, the Republican counsel did not participate in later actions. That evening, by 10-1 and 9-2 partisan votes, the joint committee announced that they would recommend that Goebel be made governor and Beckham lieutenant governor. Faced with the certainty of legislative endorsement of that stand—the shooting of Goebel had unified uncertain Democrats—Taylor acted.

The committee made their announcement at 8:00 P.M. An hour later, the Republican governor issued a proclamation that adjourned the General Assembly to meet again in London, Kentucky in a week. He based his authority to act in this manner on a clause in the constitution which said the legislature must meet in Frankfort, "except in case of war, insurrection and pestilence." Insurrection, according to Taylor, had occurred. Constitutionally, the governor's action was of questionable legality. But if he hoped to keep his office, delay might be the only recourse. A week could yield needed time, and meeting in London gave a favorable environment for Republican legislators.

And besides, Taylor was afraid. Almost certainly he expected a retaliatory attempt on his own life and the lives of his family. Taylor ordered thirty troops to guard his wife and children in the Executive Mansion. He remained on the Capitol grounds, surrounded by about 500 soldiers. The Louisville Legion and the 2d Regiment had arrived quickly following the news of the shooting and had brought with them several Gatling guns, which now faced outward toward the rest of Frankfort. In his quarters a secluded, isolated, besieged Taylor looked out on a hostile town. Below him poorly clothed troops shivered in the falling snow, awaiting the morning.

At ten o'clock the next day members of the legislature came to the Capitol, to test Taylor's proclamation. Republican Adjutant General D. R. Collier, vehemently anti-Goebel, read the order from the building's famous double spiral staircase and told legislators that they could enter only to remove personal effects. Speaker Trimble called on Democrats to meet at the Frankfort Opera House. Collier firmly reminded them that any such assembly would violate the proclamation and thus be illegal. Several legislators followed Trimble. Soldiers' bayonets refused them entrance at the Opera House. They moved toward the courthouse as troops raced to the destination first. By the time the solons reached there, a line of soldiers met them. A crowd began to talk of storming the building, but the legislators quietly withdrew. Republican members meanwhile heard the proclamation and began to leave for London.

Determined Democrats denied that any state of insurrection existed. The only danger came from Republicans, they insisted. To adopt the committee report required a joint session, yet no public building large enough could be obtained because of the soldiers. But Goebel must be declared governor and Taylor must be ousted.

Later in the afternoon word came privately to each Democratic member to meet in the Capitol Hotel that evening. The instructions asked them to assemble separately, not in groups, and then to come one by one to a second floor room. A legislator present at the time later recalled how "the lights at the meeting were dimmed and the proceedings carried on in low tone of voice." A quorum of nineteen senate Democrats and fifty-three from the house was announced as present, though those attending were not certain of the numbers. The group then heard the joint committee report, adopted it unanimously, and declared William Goebel the rightful governor. It had been less than thirty-six hours since he was shot.

Sometime before nine o'clock that same evening of 31 January 1900, Chief Justice James H. Hazelrigg of the Court of Appeals swore in Goebel as governor. Although rumors still are heard that he gave the oath to a dead man, the presence of several witnesses and the later testimony of many prominent people indicate that Goebel was still very much alive. He signed, probably with the guiding hand of others aiding him, a proclamation designed by Democrats to counter Taylor's. Goebel ordered the troops removed and the legislature reassembled.

Seal of Kentucky—Revised
Minneapolis Journal, February 1, 1900

Now began the long and involved question of who was legally governor. Was Taylor's proclamation constitutional? Was the crisis an insurrection? If so, did that void the Democratic legislative actions? Republicans kept possession of the state buildings and refused to acknowledge Democratic actions, while their opposition issued orders as if they controlled the executive office. Neither side's partisans accepted the actions of the other. Anti-Goebel leaders now faced a difficult decision. They had counselled throughout that the law should be followed, that decisions should be respected, as in the election board's 2-1 vote. And although the Democratic action might not be fair, it was apparently legal. Even Taylor admitted this, in part, when he commented that the proceedings to oust him were conducted with respect to "the formalities of the law. But it is the mere formality that is respected." Democrat Breckinridge in the *Morning Herald* soon wrote of the controversy as the "battle of truth against sham forms of law," but he recognized his side's slipping legal position. Other Republicans and anti-Goebel Democrats seemed uncertain of their course, and several believed Taylor's proclamation was unconstitutional. Yet they would not yield and allow Goebel to become their governor.

What a Lexington paper called the possible "horrors of civil and fraternal war" threatened. A random shot might have provoked bloodshed and another "Brothers' War." Taylor would not leave his quarters and guards escorted his family to visit him, a virtual prisoner. In Frankfort over 1,000 troops had assembled, and equal numbers of armed Democrats stood ready. Rockcastle County Republicans pledged to send their "full quota to the front," and followers in other counties vowed to march upon the capital if they were needed to enforce the governor's orders. Various Republican newspapers questioned the legislative proceedings that resulted in Goebel's swearing-in, which they suggested was grounds enough for disobedience.

To meet this latter objection, Democrats met on Friday and more carefully reenacted the earlier proceedings. All was still done with lights dimmed and voices low. Then Goebel took the oath of office again, with local Circuit Judge James E. Cantrill administering it. Beckham took the oath for lieutenant governor and issued an order removing Adjutant General Collier, who followed only Republican commands. Collier ignored the order, and Democratic choice John Breckinridge Castleman set up his own militia in town, subject only to the Democrats. Two governments and two armies now existed.

And in the Capitol Hotel the man indirectly responsible for this situation lay dying. William Goebel's condition fluctuated, but physicians promised little hope. Uremic poisoning set in, blood filled his lungs, pneumonia developed. Conscious most of the time, Goebel kept asking for water, but he could get little relief. Doctors gave more injections to halt pain. In times of relative painlessness, Goebel conferred with lieutenants, a politician to the end. He gave advice on possible courses of action. But he had little strength and such occurrences came less often. By 2 February his temperature had risen and his pulse had almost doubled. A newspaper reported that he had been kept alive through the night only by "artificial stimulants."

Arthur had arrived soon after the assassination attempt, gone into his brother's room and kissed him; he seldom left William alone after that. Goebel's sister came also. Justus was rushing eastward on a train from Arizona while his brother continued to fight death.

On 3 February William Goebel's struggle ended. At ten o'clock that morning he became worse. Doctors injected morphine and other drugs and administered oxygen, but they could not halt a rising fever. Hiccoughs and nausea increased in strength. Although only semiconscious, Goebel told a minister, "I do not hold myself in open violation to the word of God." In early afternoon, he asked a physician if he would die. The doctor told him he had but a few hours left. At 5:45 Goebel requested a drink of water, and then soon lapsed into unconsciousness. Twenty-five minutes later, doctors left him with his brother and sister. Alone with two of the few people who knew him well, William Goebel died at about 6:44 P.M. His brother Justus's arrival at the station within the hour came too late. At age forty-four, his ambition to be governor realized for only three days, William Goebel had survived an assassin's bullet for only a little over 100 hours.

His last words—as reported by Democrats—insured that his memory would live on: "Tell my friends to be brave, fearless and loyal to the great common people."

9

THE SEARCH FOR
THE ASSASSIN

THE LEGEND had begun. Irvin Cobb recalled later that journalists immediately scoffed at Goebel's deathbed oratory. Suspicious because William Goebel had given little evidence of such eloquence in life, he and other reporters had inquired and found that these were not the words uttered. According to Cobb's version, Goebel had craved a favorite dish and, after eating it, had told a physician before becoming unconscious, "Doc, that was a damned bad oyster." Goebel may have told his friends to be "loyal to the great common people," but more likely he did not. Initial accounts did not contain this statement. What had probably occurred was that this speech was but the first of many later moves by Democrats to insure that Goebel would become a popular martyr. A man disliked by so many would be transformed into an honored hero who nobly fought for the comman man and for the good of his party, against an evil monopoly and a militaristic opposition. The Kentucky senate adopted a resolution which said, "As the Christ's life was sacrificed to class hatred conspiring with imperial power, so the life of William Goebel paid forfeit to a conspiracy of monopolistic power."

Goebel's death removed the single barrier to reasonable discussion between the two sides. The shock of the assassination and the threat of civil war brought leaders to work for some kind of settlement. After being appointed by Beckham, Adjutant General Castleman conferred with his opposite number and longtime friend, General Collier. Both belonged to the Masonic order and agreed to honor the "brotherhood and fraternity" of the Masonic code. They pledged not to oppose each other by arms. As he left, Castleman said, "Thank God for this, for now the law and not the rifle shall determine the right." And so it would. On 5 February the Democratic majority met in Louisville, thus removing from Frankfort another potential catalyst of trouble. In London the Republican minority failed to get a quorum, as the two legislatures continued to act as if each did not exist. Yet the distance separating the antagonists allowed others to attempt compromise.

On the Sunday following Goebel's death the Democratic hierarchy conferred at Louisville's Seelbach Hotel. Beckham, Trimble, Ollie James, Urey Woodson, Henry Watterson, and other leaders talked until early morning. The day news of this meeting appeared, the Republican *Louisville Commercial* editorially called on Taylor to allow the legislature to meet in Frankfort. It also stressed a Republican theme for the next months: resubmit to the people in November the question of who is governor.

In a growing spirit of peace, a Republican called on Senator Blackburn to try to arrange a conference of leaders of both parties. Finally at 3:00 A.M. they decided to meet together. On 6 February 1900 the men talked for several hours and then signed an agreement. Democrats received acknowledgement that Goebel had been legally selected governor and that Beckham now was the rightful heir to the office. Republicans vowed to remove the militia from Frankfort. In return Democrats promised to grant immunity to Republican officials, to postpone legislative actions for a week, to stop contested elections for senator and representative in the General Assembly, and to provide a new "absolutely fair and nonpartisan" election law. Lieutenant Governor Marshall and "Gus" Willson were among seven prominent Republicans, and Beckham,

Blackburn, McCreary, Woodson, and Lillard were among nine Democrats, who signed the proposal.

Peace could at last come to Kentucky even before Goebel's burial—if Taylor would sign the agreement. The governor's options were decreasing. After a cabinet meeting, President McKinley had refused to send requested troops to the state and had so informed Republicans. Not a man of strong character, Taylor vacillated. A visitor thought he "displayed extreme distress of mind." Taylor believed he had been elected, and he wanted to hold what he thought was his rightful office. Yet he feared that if he did not resign he might be killed.

According to one description, Taylor "walked the floor, his bony arms flailing the air, the skirts of his dismal coat flapping like black distress flags, his famous underslung jaw adroop until it seemed ready to . . . fall off, and his haggard eyes streaming." Political advisor Breckinridge wrote his daughter about the man he defended: "Taylor," he said, "is an irresolute, unstable and indecisive man—incapable of either making up his mind or keeping it made up. . . . He is patriotic, well meaning and perhaps with physical courage; but wholly unfit for leadership in times like these. He advises with every body, sends for every body; seems to agree with the last advice. . . . I am sorry for him." Breckinridge judged his man well, and apparently he or Basil Duke gave the last advice. Both rejected yielding to Goebel Democrats, and Taylor followed that course when he refused to sign the peace proposal. "No Compromise With Dishonor," the *Louisville Commercial* taunted Watterson. The controversy continued for several more months.

But clearly something had to be done. *Harper's Weekly* called the time in the commonwealth, "the greatest political crisis in any State . . . since the days of 1877." The prospect of bloodshed, said the writer, "is not remote." About the only humor in a grim situation came from Mr. Dooley (F. P. Dunne), who had Taylor saying that martial law was "made undher me own personal supervision. . . . So th' nex' ye hear th' sojers ar-re chasin' th' coorts out iv th' State, th' Legislature is meetin' in Duluth, Pinsacola, an' Bangor, Maine, an' a comity iv citizens, consistin' iv some iv th' best gun-fighters iv th' State, ar-re meetin' to decide how th' controversay can be decided without loss iv blood or jobs." He ended with the observation that "they's something wr-rong in Kentucky, Hinnissy. We were too slow. Th' inimy got th' first cheat."

The object of Dooley's ridicule, Taylor on 10 February removed all but some 200 militia from the capital, as proof of his good faith, and on the nineteenth the legislature reconvened in Frankfort. But in their farcical actions in the chambers they proved worthy of Mr. Dooley's ridicule. Republican Lieutenant Governor Marshall's orders were followed only by his party, and Democrats obeyed only their acting officers. Separate prayers, separate journals, separate votes all went on at the same time, with neither side admitting the other's legitimacy. Then on the twenty-first, Taylor, Marshall, and other Republicans finally agreed to let the judiciary decide the issue. Beckham signed the proposal, which said that both parties "will submit to and abide by all orders and judgements of the courts."

The various legal actions were consolidated and went before Louisville Circuit Court Judge Emmet Field. He heard Taylor's attorneys, including Bradley, assert that the illegal "rump" General Assembly had acted in a quasi-judicial manner and had disfranchised thousands of voters by their actions. Democrats simply said that such legislative actions historically were not subject to judicial review. Judge Field supported the Democratic contention, by implication saying that insurrection had not occurred. Legislative actions "must be taken as absolute"; the court had no authority to go behind the legislative record. Republicans quickly appealed. On 6 April 1900 the Court of Appeals supported the lower court in a nonpartisan decision. That left Republicans dependent on the United States Supreme Court.

Taylor remarked: "I am not a criminal, neither shall I be a fugitive from justice. Whenever indicted, if such an outrage should be committed, I will appear for trial." But as the day came for the announcement of the final judicial decision, he suddenly went to Louisville. There a reporter found him walk-

Great Bluffs Run in the Same Channel
Chicago Chronicle, February, 1900

ing back and forth in his familiar long black coat, string tie, and black hat. "I will stay here and fight. I will not run away," he repeated as he paced. The news came quickly on 21 May 1900 that only Kentuckian John M. Harlan supported him; all the other justices saw no federal issues involved and returned the case. Fearing arrest, the now former governor fled across the river to Indiana. Taylor never returned, despite extradition efforts. He practiced law in Indianapolis until his death twenty-eight years later. The Republicans had lost the governorship.

Taylor wired his adjutant general to "surrender your office to your successor" and to dismiss the militia. Beckham soon took over the state offices. The State Board of Election Commissioners, sitting as a contest board, had earlier ruled Democrats the victors in the minor offices. Throwing out the Jefferson County vote and that of four mountain counties, they gave the Democrats a majority. The Court of Appeals by a partisan 4-3 vote affirmed that decision. (Eventually Republicans won one position.) By 22 May 1900 the matter had been settled. No more militia marched, no dual government contested for power, and all was relatively quiet.

Although some Republicans expectedly raged over the outcome, the party as a whole took the decision peacefully. They perhaps felt some guilt over the assassination, certainly recognized their minority status in both legislative and judicial branches, and, most importantly, firmly believed that the November election would put Republicans back in power. Calm acceptance of the outcome could be better received if they could regain the offices in only six months. The question of who was governor was settled—for the time.

But the question of who had killed Goebel was not. That matter troubled contemporaries for many years and has plagued those who have studied the events ever since. The day of the shooting a heavily armed man named Holland Whittaker, from Taylor's Butler County, was seized and charged with the assassination. It was the first arrest. Soon a large number of lawyers, detectives, and other investigators began to become involved as the search for Goebel's killer widened. The legislature appropriated $100,000 for the effort—which Republicans charged was used to bribe witnesses. The opposition vehemently denied the accusation. Politics had quickly found its way into the investigation and would remain. Before it ended, twenty persons were accused as principals or accessories to the assassination and sixteen of these were indicted. Three became prosecution witnesses on promises of immunity from prosecution, and of the remaining thirteen, only five went before a jury. Three convictions finally resulted.

Preliminary evidence gathered by investigations made it unlikely that the first man arrested—Whittaker—had fired the shot. Besides that, Democrats suspected—and perhaps hoped—that Republicans higher in administration circles were involved. On 9 March a clerk in the auditor's office was arrested, and warrants were issued for a former Republican secretary of state, a state police captain, Secretary of State Caleb Powers, and Powers's brother John. One of the four fled to Indiana, another to South America. Disguised in army uniforms, Powers and the fourth man boarded a train in an attempt to escape. At Lexington they were discovered and arrested. In their possession officers found a document signed by Taylor pardoning Powers for any "alleged complicity" in the murder of William Goebel. Democrats refused to honor the pardon, since they accepted only Beckham's authority. More arrests, of lesser figures, soon followed.

On 2 April 1900 Judge James E. Cantrill convened the Franklin County grand jury. "The Judge with 'flowing' whiskers" had been a former Democratic legislator and lieutenant governor, and had aided the Goebel cause since the election. He was not a nonpartisan observer, as his rulings would reveal. In the jury selection fate certainly seemed to favor Goebel Democrats, for ten of the twelve chosen jurors supported that party. Nine votes were needed for indictment, and in the end the prosecution got ten. Republicans began a charge they would continue throughout many trials—that the jury was "packed." The grand jury indicted ten men, including the three who would eventually be found guilty—Henry E.

Youtsey of the auditor's office, James B. Howard from eastern Kentucky, and Secretary of State Powers. Later indictments named William S. Taylor, among others, but he had left the state by that time.

Chief interest thus focused on Caleb Powers, the highest Republican official on trial. On 9 July 1900 his case began in Scott County after a stern and determined Judge Cantrill granted a change of venue. Still, Democrats controlled the sheriff's office, which selected and summoned prospective jurors. Former Governor Brown led a Republican-funded defense; but after exhausting challenges, he had to accept a jury of at least eleven Goebel Democrats.

While Commonwealth's Attorney Robert B. Franklin titularly led the prosecution, Justus and Arthur Goebel engaged attorney Thomas C. Campbell. A well-known lawyer from Cincinnati and New York, he received, according to Woodson, about $150,000 for services and expenses. Campbell—with few restraints by Judge Cantrill—evoked in lurid terms the Democratic version of events through the testimony of over sixty witnesses. The commonwealth sought to show that Powers brought the "mountain army" to Frankfort to intimidate the legislature and, failing that, to kill Goebel; that the secretary of state tried to entice others to do the deed earlier; that he made plans through Youtsey to accomplish the assassination and left his office key with him; and that the killer shot from a window in Powers's office.

Conflicts quickly developed. Witnesses on the scene that January day had given different accounts as to where the shot had come from, although now they generally proclaimed that Powers's office had in fact been the site. A bullet found in a nearby tree ten days after the shooting was thought to be the one that had killed Goebel, and a surveyor employed by the prosecution used it to trace an angle back to Powers's office as well. Taylor's private secretary testified as to Youtsey's actions. He had seen the man some days earlier, looking out a window, with a rifle in his hand. "If trouble comes, I am going to be prepared," Youtsey had said.

The prosecution explained Powers's absence from Frankfort

the day of the assassination as a planned move to provide a convenient alibi. (He had received word of the shooting on board a train just outside Louisville.) A witness told of an earlier plan to give a key to a proposed assassin. That, said the state, explained why the door to Powers's office was locked when men tried to enter it after the assassination. Three former aides to Powers gave the most sensational accounts. Freed from prosecution in return for their testimony, they told details of conversations in which Powers had told them to bring armed men to Frankfort to kill Democratic legislators and Goebel, to start riots, and to call out the militia to keep Republicans in office. Powers had masterminded the plot, they said.

The defense demonstrated fairly conclusively that one witness had perjured himself and that another's testimony was of questionable validity. The commonwealth's most damaging evidence had come from Powers's close associate Wharton Golden. Brown noted Golden's earlier indictments for bootlegging and carrying concealed weapons. He finally got Golden to admit reluctantly that Campbell and Arthur Goebel has harassed him and told him he would go to the penitentiary for life if he did not testify for the prosecution.

Powers took the stand himself, admitted to some rash statements, but denied the most incriminating ones attributed to him. He acknowledged bringing the 1,000 or so men to Frankfort, but cited different motives. The former secretary of state said he had both keys to his office in his possession, and explained that a duplicate must have been used. Powers vigorously asserted that he had never threatened to kill Goebel or been involved in a conspiracy to do so. He had fled because he believed partisan men would not give him a fair trial.

Other witnesses noted that shots had come from the third floor, not Powers's lower-level office, that the bullet found in the tree could not have been the one that hit Goebel, that Youtsey had acted suspiciously but quite separate from Powers. After prosecution rebuttal, the court made its charge to the jury. Cantrill's instructions were consistent with his partisanship. Twenty-four hours of lawyers' arguments sent the case to the jury, after thirty-six court days. Less than an hour later the jurors filed back into the courtroom and it was announced that—as expected—they had found Powers guilty. He was sentenced to life imprisonment. While his lawyers appealed, Powers went back to jail.

On 7 September 1900, Jim Howard's case began in Frankfort. Thirty-three years old, married and with three children, the quiet Clay County Republican had been engaged in the bitter White-Baker feud that had ended in several deaths. He had come to the capital, he said, seeking a pardon from Taylor. Democrats charged that he had been the actual assassin. Jury selection under Judge Cantrill continued the earlier patterns, as at least eleven Democrats heard the case. Several witnesses testified as to Howard's presence on the grounds of the Capitol, and five men swore that they had heard him boast that he had done the deed. Attorney Campbell brought in and dwelt on Howard's earlier indictments for murder in the Clay County feud—noting parallels. Howard also testified in his own defense, saying the he was in a hotel at the time of the shooting and denying the statements attributed to him. His defense attorney called three men who weakly supported his alibi. After the same biased instructions by Cantrill and sensational closing arguments by both sides, the jury began its deliberations. In a half hour they returned a verdict of guilty and called for the death penalty. An appeal followed.

A third trial opened in Scott County before Judge Cantrill on 8 October 1900. Goebel Democrat jurors again were selected to hear the case. The defendant was Henry E. Youtsey. A religious man from a respected family, the stenographer from Newport was also rash, undisciplined, and very unstable. To Democratic eyes he had been the intermediary between Powers and Howard. A vengeful Arthur Goebel took the stand. In appearance resembling his oldest brother, both eloquent and forceful, he dramatically told how the defendant had admitted guilt to him. Youtsey sprang up and shouted, "That's a lie. I hope God will kill me if I ever said a word to that man or he to me." The judge ordered him to sit down. He refused to do so. "There is no blood on my hands, not a particle. I want everybody to see it. I am innocent." As deputies tried to restrain him, Youtsey fell to the floor. He sobbed and shouted, seemed to faint, and could not be revived. The next day doctors told the court that Youtsey was "temporarily deranged," and during the rest of the trial the defendant lay as if lifeless on a cot brought daily into the courtroom.

After the delay Arthur Goebel testified that Youtsey had admitted to him that he had consulted then governor Taylor about the matter of William Goebel. Taylor told him to carry out his plans. He then met Howard outside Powers's locked office, gave him the key and some special cartridges (to penetrate the bullet proof vest they thought Goebel wore), and left. Other evidence introduced confirmed Youtsey's purchase of some specially made bullets. Defense attorneys could not call on their client, who remained unconscious, and Howard's statement that he had never met Youtsey had little force. In less than an hour, the jury found Youtsey guilty. Within a few days Youtsey recovered completely. (He later acknowledged that he had faked the coma "because it seemed to be the best thing I could do.") He did not appeal the verdict and began serving his life sentence. The Democrats had their assassins; the Republicans now had their own martyrs.

When the two appeals—Howard's and Powers's—reached the Court of Appeals, a change had occurred in the composition of the court. Republican Edward C. O'Rear had won election to what had been a Democratic seat. The men faced judges who were 4-3 Republican. Not surprisingly, the appellate court, by that partisan vote, reversed both cases and sent them back for new trials. The majority cited Cantrill's "prejudiced" rulings regarding admission of evidence, his charge to the jury, and use of Howard's past record in the Clay County murders. And so began the long process of trials that continued for seven more years. Howard went through two more trials, Powers three. With the exception of Powers's last trial, "packed" juries remained the rule—of 368 jurors summoned in one, only 8 were Republican, from counties over 40 percent Republican. In another, Powers saw 173 of the 176 men summoned as Goebel Democrats.

Testimony in earlier trials had been reprinted in newspapers across the state and finding an unbiased jury was almost an impossibility. Samuel Hopkins Adams's view of the atmosphere in Kentucky expressed the temper surrounding each trial: "How deeply the bitterness of the Goebel killing has entered into the life of Kentucky no outsider can fully realize. The animosities engendered by it have brought about literally scores of fatal quarrels. Business partnerships have been dissolved; churches have been disrupted; lifelong friendships have been withered; families have been split; there is no locality so remote, no circle so closely knit, as to escape the evil influence. At the Capital of the state people dare not talk freely about it."

Howard's second trial began in January 1902 with arguments and judicial instructions almost identical to the first. The only change in the outcome was that his guilty conviction brought with it life imprisonment rather than the death penalty. He appealed, and the court again reversed the results by a partisan vote. Democrats refused to allow to go free men they saw as murderers and conspirators. Howard's third trial began in April 1903. Only this time a new prosecution witness testified. Henry Youtsey had been in the penitentiary for two years now, and reporters described his wild, furtive eyes, and his prison pallor. Some reports circulated that he had been tortured; more likely he appeared on promises of leniency. Whatever the cause, Youtsey was a firm friend of the prosecution.

Youtsey linked Taylor to the "conspiracy" by saying that the ex-governor had discussed the planned assassination with Howard and himself. According to Youtsey, Taylor and Powers planned it, he served as their aide, and Howard fired the shot. The defense cross-examined Youtsey effectively, indicated some obvious errors, introduced Taylor's deposition that he had never talked to Howard or suggested assassination, and allowed Powers and Howard to take the stand and deny Youtsey's version. But the results revealed the futility of defense: Howard was found guilty. The usual appeal followed. But an election had once again changed the complexion of the court. Now 5-2 Democratic, the Kentucky Court of Appeals on 22 April 1904 affirmed Howard's conviction by that partisan margin. A year and a half later, the United States Supreme Court refused to review that decision. In 1906 Howard joined Youtsey and began serving a life sentense.

Powers had faced similar experiences. His second trial had begun in October 1901 with two of his prominent accusers now absent. Both witnesses had repudiated their previous testimony, citing bribery and intimidation. Republicans immediately seized on this as proof of their accusation of a political witch hunt, while Democrats said the opposition simply had bribed these men to change their stories. Nevertheless, the trial went much as the first one, with Cantrill's same partisan tactics. And at the end the jury returned the same verdict and punishment as before. Power's appeal was successful.

The third trial might prove crucial. Powers faced this confrontation with the knowledge of Youtsey's damaging testimony. He knew the prosecution sought the death sentence. He perhaps guessed that reversal by an unfriendly Court of Appeals was unlikely. A guilty verdict this time might mean his life. Powers prepared thoroughly and engaged the services of new counsel, including Lexington attorney Samuel M. Wilson. His lawyers asked Cantrill to disqualify himself, in accord with what the appellate court had ruled in its last reversal. Cantrill refused. Finally, after Powers's lawyers obtained a court mandate ordering his disqualification, an angry judge obeyed rather than face contempt charges. The new judge had also supported Goebel, but his overall rulings were less partial than Cantrill's.

In August 1903—over three years since his first trial—Caleb Powers faced the prosecution again. The same evidence was given, aided this time by Youtsey's more detailed testimony. In much better health now—the defense attempted to show a cause and effect relationship brought about by his testimony—Youtsey again implicated Taylor, Powers, and

121

Howard. All three men, in person or by deposition, refuted his story. After thirty-eight days of hearing evidence, the respective counsels made their appeals. Then Powers rose.

Trained in the law, speaking only with the briefest notes, he made an able and emotional talk that lasted seven hours. Widely reprinted later, it covers over eighty pages of fine print. Whether a conspirator or not, Powers was a very capable and intelligent man. After reading over his address one student of the trials wrote that Powers's speech was "so completely objective that at times it was difficult to realize he was talking of and for himself and not for someone else."

Powers analyzed the evidence, stressed the weaknesses of the prosecution's case, emphasized the partisanship involved, and argued his defense. All agree on the cowardliness of assassination, he said, all agree that "the killing of Goebel was the worst possible thing that could have befallen the Republican party," all agree that the murderer should be punished. "We differ as to who is responsible for his death." Point by point he went over the testimony, carefully stressing strong points, skillfully omitting weak ones. He ended with a melodramatic portrayal of his mother at home awaiting a verdict. "With a frail and trembling hand she moves back the white hair from her sorrow-ridden brow," went a sample sentence. And then he asked the jury "to liberate the suffering innocent and send an outraged boy back to the country he loves."

The masterful, if at times overdramatic, speech left the majority of the courtroom in tears. Even jurors cried, according to some accounts, but emotion did not sway their votes. The verdict was guilty. As Campbell had asked, they rendered a punishment of death. If the appellate court ruled against Powers in his appeal, he would be hanged. But in a rare nonpartisan move during these very partisan trials, two Democrats joined two Republicans and reversed the lower court. They cited errors in Campbell's passionate closing argument for the death penalty and the partisan jury selection as bases for their decision.

Still no relief came to Caleb Powers. His clever, effective, and excellent autobiography *My Own Story* earned him some wealth and much sympathy when it appeared in 1905. But in late November 1907 his fourth trial began. Prosecutor Campbell had died and thus would harass him no more. On the other hand, Judge Cantrill had been elected to the Court of Appeals, where his influence would do the Republicans' cause no good. Nevertheless, with Campbell dead and Cantrill not involved at the lower court level, a more general spirit of justice prevailed. The fact that a Republican had just been elected governor may have helped.

Whatever the cause, jury selection went well for Powers, with eight Republicans and four Democrats being chosen. The defense introduced witnesses who tended to discredit Youtsey's testimony. Their statements suggested that Youtsey himself had fired the shot. One man swore that he had taken a Marlin rifle from Powers's office the day of the assassination and he produced what he said was the weapon used to kill Goebel. Youtsey had sold the rifle to a man not implicated in the affair, but the former owner knew its whereabouts that January day in 1900. Now almost eight years later, on 2 January 1908, Powers's case went to a jury once again. After two days' deliberation the jurors deadlocked and both sides consented to dismiss them. Reporters announced that the vote had been 10-2 for acquittal.

Both Howard and Powers petitioned the Republican governor for a pardon. On 13 June 1908, "Gus" Willson stated his belief that both men were innocent, and that Youtsey, now a thoroughly discredited Republican, had killed Goebel. No conspiracy existed, said the governor. Less than a year later, Willson issued pardons to six other men, including former Governor Taylor. "The American Dreyfus," as Powers was being called, had, like Howard, been imprisoned for over eight years when freed. Democrats regained the governorship in 1911, and five years later Youtsey was paroled. Democratic Governor James D. Black—from Powers's Knox County— granted the last of the three convicted men a full pardon in 1919. After two decades the controversy over who had killed Goebel was almost over.

Youtsey lived for a time as a forlorn and rejected man, divorced by his wife and with few friends. He eventually remarried and served as county clerk. Howard went into seclusion in Clay County, refused to see most visitors, and said almost nothing further about his role in the affair. He did happen to be in Georgetown the day of old enemy Judge Cantrill's funeral. Someone asked him if he wanted to attend. "No," he answered, "but I am willing for it to be known that his funeral has my hearty endorsement." Up to his death, Howard proclaimed his innocence.

Powers received a vindication of sorts. As he liked to say, he served as many years in Congress as he had in jail. Republicans, certain of his persecution by Democrats, selected him over the party's incumbent in the 1910 primary and swept him to victory in the fall. Three times Powers won reelection to the House, although his congressional record was not outstanding. Powers died in 1932, aged sixty-four, a private man who, to the last, never diverged from his defense of years earlier.

Who, then, assassinated William Goebel? No simple answer can be given. If the court testimony is accepted uncritically a solid scheme of plots, planned assassinations, and wholesale murders can be outlined. It is easy to paint a believable picture of a conspiracy involving Powers, Youtsey, Howard, and others—easy but not quite fair. The testimony is too unreliable, the partisanship too strong. Perjured evidence was known at the time, and other sworn statements may be equally faulty. As a writer for *Harper's Weekly* wrote in 1900, "One side charges too much; the other side denies too much."

Many have examined the case and found their own villains. A relative was certain that his cousin Youtsey was the assassin; Powers's attorney Wilson agreed; Urey Woodson, author of a book on Goebel, firmly believed Howard guilty. Others had their own culprits. Of the known possibilities Howard, who had killed before, seems a good choice—with Youtsey as an accomplice. Youtsey, too, had the temperament of an assassin. And it is conceivable that somewhere lived an unknown man, alone in the knowledge that he had killed a governor.

It may be begging the question, but the evidence is simply too contradictory and the people involved were too partisan to allow any definitive answer. Until new information is uncovered, the answer to the question, "Who killed William Goebel?" is simply, "We do not know." Nor may we ever.

10

"HE IS GOEBEL, THAT IS ALL"

ALTHOUGH GOEBEL was the only American governor who died in office as a result of an assassination—among the roughly 1300 who have served—he was not the victim of a unique act. Before him in 1893, the Kentucky-born mayor of Chicago had been shot. In 1901 President McKinley was killed, and eleven years later Theodore Roosevelt was wounded by a would-be assassin. In Tennessee former United States Senator and recently defeated gubernatorial nominee Edward Ward Carmack died of wounds suffered in a 1908 shooting. In Kentucky itself the violent spirit of the "dark and bloody ground" had resulted earlier in the death of a Court of Appeals justice and in various other murders.

But if Goebel's assassination occurred in a framework of violence it was different in other ways. Studies have indicated that many attacks on political leaders were directed more at the office held or sought than at the person. In Goebel's case it seems fairly certain that the man himself provoked the action. Goebel fits well the category of "high risk" politicians—men who excessively drive themselves to advance their careers, while willingly exposing themselves to dangerous situations.

Goebel's own behavior aroused intense hatred and bitter reaction. Convinced that uncorrected evils existed, Goebel increasingly pictured himself as the target of organized political plots, as the lone figure fighting a sinister opposition: his course became more correct, his opponents' less defensible. Goebel almost had to have this view in order to drive himself to the lengths required for victory. Ambition united with a reform obsession, and the two became inseparable. Compromise could not be accepted in Goebel's political morality play.

T. Harry Williams's appraisal of Huey Long—a different type of leader—applies also to Goebel: "He wanted to do good, but to accomplish that he had to have power. So he took power, and finally the means and the end became so entwined in his mind that he could not distinguish between them, could not tell whether he wanted power as a method or for its own sake." Thus Goebel moved in ways that made him appear more dangerous to the established order than any previous state politician. His actions strengthened his opponents' view of him as an utterly ruthless man who would use any means— legal or not—to win office. They felt his tactics dictated their responses. When Goebel appeared near his goal, a minority angered by events provided the "Lost Cause" environment from which the assassin probably emerged. Viewed as a corrupt political boss, Goebel could be seen by an enemy as a menace that must be removed.

Goebel's ambition had forced him to the course of machine politician, and he initiated the events that turned him into "Boss Bill, the Kenton King." He recognized that to achieve his desires would require less traditional methods—a dangerous gambit in a conservative state. In an attempt to overthrow the established party machinery he built his own machine in a ruthless manner. Not to do this meant less opportunity for final victory. And so he irreversibly committed his career to controversy—and eventually to violence.

In retrospect, William Goebel appears as a prototype of the twentieth-century urban political boss with a reform orientation. To contemporaries in Kentucky this appearance was a contradiction they could not understand: Goebel had either to be a boss or a reformer; he could not be both. Within a few decades of his death, however, Goebel's actions did not seem so unusual. His railroad bills and election law varied little from the prevailing southern pattern. Men like "Billy" Klair of Lexington, Mickey Brennan of Louisville, and Maurice Galvin of Covington continued his political type in Kentucky. "Boss" Ed Crump of Memphis operated in a similar fashion. Other urban machines, such as New Orleans' "Old Regulars," rose to power as the South became less rural-oriented. By the early twentieth century various "machines" operated in almost every southern state. Nor were leaders of the Progressive movement immune to machine influences. Woodrow Wilson used New Jersey bosses in his career, for example. But in Goebel's era, in Kentucky's environment, his association with boss rule turned many articulate reformers against him and made his task more difficult.

This was the contradiction: while Goebel voiced the reform refrain, his actions spoke against reform. Other leaders of the time—"Golden Rule" Jones of Toledo and Kentucky-born Tom Johnson of Cleveland, for example—also attacked organized wealth and corporations. But they directed their efforts against political machines as well. Goebel's stands paralleled and anticipated many of the programs of Robert M. LaFollette—equalization of corporate property, regulation of railroad rates, and strong commissions. But when LaFollette found opponents blocking his every step, he countered by taking his programs to the people, and his resonant voice and speaking ability allowed him to articulate his thoughts. Wilson did the same in New Jersey. In both cases the masses reacted favorably. Goebel had to influence through his governmental actions, and if his way was blocked, his personality and oratory did not easily allow him to appeal successfully to the people.

Convincing himself that he sought noble goals, Goebel recognized that the political world counted only votes, not intentions. And in his effort to control Kentucky he went to excessive lengths, disrupted his party, and almost caused civil war in the state. Goebel died trying to gain power, in some ways a victim of himself, a man sacrificed to ambition without limit and politics without compromise.

Assassinations have changed public attitudes and influenced subsequent political history. In Goebel's case the question arose quickly: would his death end reform in the state? Some historians have suggested that the assassination did in fact crush the progressive spirit, and that as a result Kentucky never experienced the reforms of the Progressive Era. In one sense this view is correct. For the assassination warned would-be reformers of the dangers of attempting too much, of challenging the established order too forcefully.

Overall, however, the murder of William Goebel did not abort reform. Constructive change did come to the commonwealth. The fact that it came slowly and with less force than elsewhere owes more to the state's relative poverty, rurality, and continued legacy of violence than to one man's assassination. Actually many specific changes advocated by Goebel came about quite quickly and the Progressive movement did find a willing—if belated—home in Kentucky.

Reform began in the Democratic rump assembly that ruled following the assassination. Though without Republican participation, this General Assembly was recognized as legal by the courts. It quickly enacted the McChord bill without a dissenting vote, giving the Railroad Commission power "to make and fix a just and reasonable rate." Another act—to go into effect at once because "armed hordes of men have been transported to Frankfort"—made illegal such free transportation "for the purpose of intimidating any office or officers in this Commonwealth." A third act struck out at corporations' involvement in elections by forbidding such organizations to furnish "any money, privilege, favor or other thing of value to any political or quasi political organization." From the grave William Goebel had won his victories over the railroads.

Goebel's youthful successor has been uniformly reprehended for his inability to continue this reform spirit. J. C. W. Beckham allowed his attention and efforts to focus on a bloody mountain feud and on lawless Night Rider activity in the Black Patch War. In both cases he appeared to side with violence. His legislature passed a law segregating Berea College, which created a brief furor. And by the end of his term, the governor came under attack for "selling out" to the L & N. Yet despite these less than distinguished actions, Beckham did continue—sporadically—the reform spirit suggested by Goebel. His administration extended the school term, set up an effective compulsory education law, began two teachers' colleges, successfully amended the Food and Drug Act, raised the age of consent, passed a child labor law, and began construction of a much needed new capitol.

In fact, it is at least possible that Goebel would not have greatly improved upon Beckham's record had he lived. His dozen years in the senate had not resulted in many specific legislative acts that bore his stamp. The Goebel Election Law had been far from legitimate reform, for instance. Beckham got it repealed before the special 1900 election (which he barely won). And while Goebel had kept before the people some important questions, he had shown only limited interest in others, such as educational reform. Goebel never had the opportunity to show whether he would foster major reform once in control of government or simply reach for more power, as enemies charged. But his death stimulated a brief flurry of reform legislation that helped accomplish his program. The assassination did not snuff out the growing flame of progressivism.

The sparks kindled during Beckham's seven years in office burst into a relative inferno of reform when the Democrats regained the gubernatorial office in 1911 after Willson's term. It was under the administration of cautious, conservative ex-Confederate "Bothsides" McCreary that progressivism came to Kentucky in full force. He had used his remarkable political ability to regain the governor's chair, and he followed—typically—voters ready for constructive change. As a result McCreary ended his four years with a generally good record of reform.

Leaders opposed to Goebel at the Music Hall years before now won the prize for which they had contested in 1899. Progressivism continued its advance under Governor A. O. Stanley. Reform thus came to Kentucky slowly but ironically under the old order that Goebel had so disliked, or under the leadership of those who had opposed him before his nomination, while supporting their party after it. Many of the very forces Goebel had viewed as reactionary became in fact the vanguard of the Progressive movement. They had triumphed over Goebel.

And throughout these years William Goebel was not remembered chiefly as a reformer, or even as a political boss, but rather only as the assassinated martyr. Democratic orators cried out against "the party that murdered Goebel," and "pitiful politicians . . . ghoul-like . . . [would] metaphorically dig up his remains to excite the populace and accomplish their pitiful little ends." The ghost of the man who had rejected such appeals in the nineteenth century now became the "bloody shirt" issue of the twentieth. Thus William Goebel, who—correctly or not—could have been remembered as a symbol of reform, became instead only a campaign tactic. This perhaps was the real tragedy of Goebel.

But Goebel was more than a campaign tactic. To his contemporaries, exactly what he was depended on your political faith. To historians, he remains something of a paradox even now. Perhaps Arthur Goebel analyzed his brother best in a December 1900 letter. "It is almost a year since William died," he concluded, "and he lives in the minds of the people as much as ever. Why is it? He is Goebel, that is all."

Bibliographical Note

AN EXTENSIVE collection of Goebel letters has not yet been made public, if they exist. The best available source is the Goebel Family Letters, on microfilm in Special Collections, Margaret I. King Library, University of Kentucky. Seldom used before, these are a rich source of information. Acknowledgement is made to Dr. Bennett Wall of Tulane University for his role in gathering these and other manuscripts.

For Goebel's early life and background see the small William Goebel Papers at the University of Kentucky, his father's Compiled Service Record at the National Archives, and Kenton County Tax Lists in the Kentucky Historical Society. Kenton County Will Book 8 has Goebel's will. The John White Stevenson Collection, at the University of Kentucky, gives insights into Goebel's mentor.

In the politics of the 1890s much more is available from the side that opposed Goebel. Covington rivals speak out in the Hallam Family Papers and the Mackoy Family Papers while the Preston-Johnston Family Papers, the W. J. Stone Papers, the Cassius Marcellus Clay Collection, and the Lindsay Family Papers offer much material. Valuable information on railroads can be discovered in the Craig Shelby Papers. All these major collections are at the University of Kentucky. At the Manuscript Division, Library of Congress, the valuable, but unwieldy collection of the Breckinridge Family Papers shows W. C. P. Breckinridge's changing politics. The Henry Watterson Papers are disappointing.

Republicans speak more softly, for less material on them is available. The Kentucky Historical Society houses the unprocessed papers of the governors of this period. The papers of both W. O. Bradley and W. S. Taylor proved helpful. Only a few items are in the William Sylvestor Taylor Papers, on microfilm at the University of Kentucky, while the William McKinley Papers at the Library of Congress, good for 1899, are surprisingly silent on events of 1900. See also the Reuben N. Miller Papers at the University of Kentucky, and William O'Connell Bradley's Scrapbooks which chiefly contain newspaper clippings.

The Filson Club in Louisville has many items that focus primarily on the election of 1899 and its aftermath. The Arthur Younger Ford Papers, the James W. Ainslie Letters, and the Dee Armstrong and William G. Harding Papers all provide items of use. Richard W. Knott's biased "History of Goebelism," in the Temple Bodley Collection, is valuable.

Information on the trials themselves can be found in the Goebel Papers at the Kentucky Historical Society, or in the Caleb Powers Trial Papers in the Wilson Manuscript Collection at the University of Kentucky. Scrapbooks of various use include the Annie G. Crutcher, J. C. W. Beckham, and W. W. Stevenson scrapbooks at the Kentucky Historical Society, and the "Clippings on the Assassination of William Goebel," Lillard H. Carter Scrapbook, and Bruce Ferguson Scrapbook, at the University of Kentucky.

Most earlier accounts concerning Goebel have relied chiefly on the Democratic *Courier-Journal*, the Lexington *Morning Herald*, and the Republican Lexington *Daily Leader*. These are all valuable and have been used here as well. But three other major dailies give a different viewpoint and are in some ways even more instructive. The *Louisville Commercial* spoke for Republicans, the Louisville *Evening Post* for independents, and the *Louisville Dispatch* for Brown Democrats in 1899. To use only these, however, risks ignoring the smaller but still influential papers. Included among the more than twenty examined, were the *Hickman Courier*, the *Hazel Green Herald*, the Nelson County *Record*, the *Glasgow Times*, the London *Mountain Echo*, the *Paducah Sun*, and the Louisville *Kentucky Irish-American*. Information on Goebel's elections and environment in Covington comes from the Newport *Kentucky State Journal* and the *Cincinnati En-*

quirer. One of the most useful out-of-state newspapers was the *New York Times*.

Goebel's senate career can be followed in the Kentucky *Senate Journals*, 1887–1900, and other events can be traced in the *House Journals* of the same period. The final results are printed in Kentucky *Acts of the General Assembly*. The massive, four-volume *Official Report of the Proceedings and Debates in the Convention . . . to adopt, amend or change the Constitution of the State of Kentucky* traces in detail Goebel's public role. *Kentucky Reports*, vol. 108, has the state court ruling on the contested election.

Surprisingly few studies of Goebel have been printed. The most exhaustive has not. William S. Lester's manuscript, "The Goebel Affair" relies on standard sources, is anti-Goebel and anti-Powers, and is over 600 pages long. It suffers from an uncritical use of the trial testimony. Perhaps the best book-length study is also the oldest one: R. E. Hughes, F. W. Schaefer, and E. L. Williams, *That Kentucky Campaign; or the Law, the Ballot and the People in the Goebel-Taylor Contest* (Cincinnati, 1900). Considering the authors' closeness to events, it is surprisingly accurate.

The same cannot be said of Urey Woodson's *First New Dealer* (Louisville, 1939), which is poorly organized as well. Its value comes from Woodson's nearness to Goebel. A more biased Republican view is E. B. Tackett's *A Review of the Goebel Tragedy* (Lexington, c. 1916).

Perhaps the first scholarly examination of Goebel came from Thomas D. Clark. In the first edition of his *History of Kentucky* (New York, 1937) and then in his "The People, William Goebel, and the Kentucky Railroad," *Journal of Southern History* 5 (1939), he gave an interpretation of Goebel that became standard. Both Professor Clark in his "William Goebel—Southern Demagogue," *University of Kentucky Research Club* 7 (1941) and Joseph G. Green in "William Goebel: Demagogue or Democrat?" *Southern Speech Journal* 27 (1961) examined their subject as a stump speaker and both found a demagogue. Brief sketches of Goebel's life are in G. Glenn Clift's *Governors of Kentucky, 1792–1942*

(Cynthiana, Ky., 1942) and Robert S. Cotterill, "William Goebel," *Dictionary of American Biography* (24 vols., New York, 1927–).

My information on the trials came in large part from Francis X. Busch, *They Escaped the Hangman* (Indianapolis and New York, 1953). See also A. F. Johnson, *Famous Kentucky Tragedies and Trials* (Louisville, 1916).

There are many good regional studies available. Two important ones are C. Vann Woodward's *Origins of the New South, 1877–1913* (Baton Rouge, 1951) and a textbook account particularly strong on the postwar South—Francis B. Simkins' and Charles P. Roland's *A History of the South* (4th rev. ed., New York, 1972).

Among the state studies, Clark's *History*, already noted, and his *Kentucky: Land of Contrast* (New York, 1968) look at events in the commonwealth in this period. Election statistics for presidential races are analyzed well in Jasper B. Shannon and Ruth McQuown, *Presidential Politics in Kentucky, 1824–1948* (Lexington, 1950). A provoking analysis of earlier politics is Thomas L. Connelly's "Neo-Confederatism or Power Vacuum: Post War Kentucky Politics Reappraised," *Register of the Kentucky Historical Society* 64 (1966). See also George Leo Willis, Sr., *Kentucky Democracy* (3 vols., Louisville, 1935), vol. 1; and a recent study by Hambleton Tapp and James C. Klotter, *Kentucky: Decades of Discord, 1865–1900* (Frankfort, 1977).

Studies of men important in Goebel's career include Arndt M. Stickles, *Simon Bolivar Buckner: Borderland Knight* (Chapel Hill, 1940); James A. Barnes, *John G. Carlisle: Financial Statesman* (New York, 1931); Joseph F. Wall, *Henry Watterson: Reconstructed Rebel* (New York, 1956); and Mary K. Bonsteel Tachau, "The Making of a Railroad President: Milton Hannibal Smith and the L & N," *Filson Club History Quarterly* 43 (1969).

Recollections of those on the scene during this period vary in usefulness. Some of the best are Caleb Powers, *My Own Story* (Indianapolis, 1905); the unreliable Irvin S. Cobb, *Exit*

Laughing (Indianapolis and New York, 1941) and *Stickfuls* (New York, 1923); John B. Castleman, *Active Service* (Louisville, 1917); and Isaac F. Marcosson, *Adventures in Interviewing* (New York, 1919). Three older histories are virtual recollections: Samuel M. Wilson's *History of Kentucky* (Chicago, 1928), vol. 2, gives Powers's chief lawyer's view. Both E. Polk Johnson, *A History of Kentucky and Kentuckians* (3 vols., Chicago and New York, 1921) and Z. F. Smith, *History of Kentucky* (rev. ed., Louisville, 1901) should be examined. Background biographical information is in *The Illustrated Centennial Record of the State of Kentucky* (Louisville, 1892); *Biographical Cyclopaedia of the Commonwealth of Kentucky* (Chicago, 1896); and H. Levin, editor, *Lawyers and Lawmakers of Kentucky* (Chicago, [1897]).

Many studies help to better understand Goebel, including William D. Miller, *Mr. Crump of Memphis* (Baton Rouge, 1964) and T. Harry Williams, *Huey Long* (New York, 1969). Useful examinations of political murder are Lauren Paine, *The Assassin's World* (New York, 1975); William J. Crolty, editor, *Assassins and the Political Order* (New York, 1971); and Hugh Davis Graham and Ted Robert Gurr, editors, *The History of Violence in America* (New York and Washington, 1969).

Among the unpublished works is an excellent 1935 senior thesis from Princeton University—Edward F. Prichard, Jr., "Popular Political Movements in Kentucky, 1875–1900." Focusing more on Goebel is Nicholas C. Burckel, "Progressive Governors in the Border States . . . 1900–1918" (Ph.D. dissertation, University of Wisconsin, 1971). Most of Burckel's chapter on Goebel was published in the *Filson Club History Quarterly* 48 (1974) as "William Goebel and the Campaign for Railroad Regulation in Kentucky." See also John D. Minton, "The Political Prosecution and Trials of Caleb Powers" (Master's thesis, University of Kentucky, 1947). James C. Klotter, "The Breckinridges of Kentucky: Two Centuries of Leadership" (Ph.D. dissertation, University of Kentucky, 1975) examines the career of W. C. P. Breckinridge.